Mothers Are People Too

Mothers Are People Too

A Contemporary Analysis of Motherhood

Anita Spencer

Paulist Press New York/Ramsey

Acknowledgement
An excerpt from *Momism: The Silent Disease of America,* by Hans Sebald, Chicago: Nelson Hall Co., 1976, is used by permission of the publisher.

Library of Congress
Catalog Card Number: 83-62946

ISBN: 0-8091-2616-8 (paper)

Published by Paulist Press
545 Island Road, Ramsey, N.J. 07446

Printed and bound in the
United States of America

Contents

Dedications

This book is dedicated to the following very special people in my life.

To my mother, Jeanne Spencer

She did not always have all the right answers and she certainly did not have all the options that I had. She may not have loved me quite as unconditionally as I wanted, but as I reflect back on her life I can truly say that she tried her hardest and did the very best she could. There is not much more for which a daughter could ask. I love you, mom.

To my three sons: Steven, Scott, and Christopher

Mothering you has been truly one of the greatest joys in my life. I once wrote a fairy tale about myself that expresses best the message that I wish to give to you.

Once upon a time there was a very special princess. She grew up always knowing that there was something very unique and life-giving about her. Even though sad and cruel things happened in her life, there was a special light that shone from within.

She married and had three handsome princes whom she loved with all her heart. As her little princes grew older she discovered that being a princess was much too confining. She was no longer content to sit in her castle all day. She wanted to stretch her wings and be all that she could be. She went against her husband's wishes and much sadness and grief came upon her. He was very angry and ran off with another. But she knew she was right and so she survived the pain and did go on to be something very much more. It was never her intent to be perfect but just to be her own uniquely special self and to become as whole and integrated as she could be.

The one great sadness in the little princess' life was that she had somehow caused her children pain. She would have spared them that if only she could. Her deepest wish was that someday her sons would come to understand what she did and see it as a beautiful legacy handed down to them by this little princess. They would then be able to grow up knowing that people can be more than what they presently are. That women and men can both grow and self-actualize. They can become whole. It was her hope that the day would come when her sons would salute her for the model that she had given them.

Introduction

Ever since writing my book *Seasons: A Woman's Search for Self Through Life's Stages,* I had been feeling a need to write a book on motherhood. I decided to delay this project because I wanted to concentrate on a study I was conducting about self-actualized women. A sense of urgency to turn my energies back to writing about motherhood ensued for me when an article appeared on the front page of several prominent newspapers. The article was about women who did not have custody of their children.

What was especially disturbing about the article was the picture on the front page. It showed a woman in a rocking chair looking devastated and alone with her head drooped down and her child's teddy bear flung over her arm. She looked as if her life was over and she had just taken an overdose of pills as a result. The article talked about two women who had attempted suicide after losing custody of their children, and the other women interviewed also felt that somehow their own lives were over now that they were no longer mothers on a full-time basis. One got a sense from the article that losing custody of children was somehow a fate worse than death and that the future held nothing positive.

These women were discouraged and disillusioned and had given up on themselves as a result.

The article left me with a very uncomfortable feeling in the pit of my stomach. It was a feeling as if someone had just played a cruel practical joke on women. My heart reached out to the mothers in the news story because I could see them as victims of a rapidly changing society. But change generally outruns consciousness. Women are now said to be equal to men in the sight of the law. That was one reason for the institution of "no fault" divorce laws in many states. When a marriage ends, the court takes everything the couple has and divides it in half and that can include the children as well. The problem is that women are still not really equal to men due to their socialization into dependency and society's expectation that they remain home and care for the husband and children. A woman is not the economic equal of a man. A "good" woman was trained to subordinate her life to her husband's. Her needs for achievement and mastery would be met vicariously through his accomplishments and those of her children.

The woman pictured in the article never dreamed that she would ever have to take care of herself or live alone. Maybe it should have occurred to her as a possibility but she'd been trained and told from infancy onward that her survival would lie in the arms of a man. It is no wonder that this woman has a look about her that death would be much more preferable than this intense agony that she is currently feeling. Her sense of being betrayed is monumental. After all, she did what she was socialized to do and she did it to the best of her ability. It is hard for her to accept what she sees as a very unjust punishment.

As a coordinator and counselor for a project for "Displaced Homemakers," I was even more upset about this article because I was concerned for the women who would read it and would see it as evidence that a woman without her motherhood role in the traditional sense was to be condemned. "Displaced Homemakers" are women who have lost their major source of financial and emotional support due to death, divorce or disability of their spouse. These women have usually not worked outside of the home and have gotten their fulfillment and value in life from being mothers and wives. This source of fulfillment has now been taken away from them usually through no fault of their own. Their plight is sad indeed.

Most of the women in this project are going through divorce and therefore the issue of who is going to get custody of the children is of great concern. Because there is "no fault" divorce in California, the custody of children is determined by who is better able to parent them. It is important to observe what is going on in California courts because California has been described as the forerunner of social trends for the rest of the nation. Joint custody is encouraged in California, but if a father wishes to fight for custody he has a good chance of succeeding if he can prove that he has more time available for the children and is financially in a better position to care for them.

Even in the cases where joint custody is the result, the woman's role as mother will change significantly. The women in my project are panicked over this issue. They tell me that if they lose the children their life will be meaningless and that they no longer will have reason to go on living. These women see themselves only as mothers and have no sense of identity beyond this role. To be any less than a full-time mother is viewed by them as having failed at motherhood. And to have failed at motherhood is to have failed the "self" in some fundamental way. The newspaper article simply reinforced society's opinion and the woman's own internal assessment of herself that women without their children are doomed to lives of pain and misery and that they deserve this agony.

The realities of life have changed dramatically in the last twenty years. A woman can no longer count on the role of motherhood to give her value as a person. Forty-seven percent of all California women who are thirty-five years of age or older are widowed or divorced. Even if divorce never becomes an actuality, children do grow up and leave home. This is especially a difficult time for older women who have focused all their energy on motherhood. The life expectancy of women in 1978 was 77.2 years of age, and therefore only a small percentage of a woman's life will be spent in active mothering. When the last child leaves home, a tremendous sense of loss is experienced if a woman has no other basis for her self-identity. All mothers have to face the empty nest syndrome and then the issue of identity and self-value must be faced. It is just that women who lose custody must face this issue sooner than most. What really concerns me is that so few women deal with this issue successfully and I have really agonized over why this is so. It is as if the problem has never been articulated in such a way that we could comprehend how essential was its resolution.

The problem is that we are living in a new era when the role of motherhood in the life of a woman has drastically changed. Most women no longer have the option of staying home and being full-time wives and mothers. If they do so they run the risk of having to economically and emotionally depend on themselves at some later point in their life and finding themselves ill equipped for the task. What is happening is that internally a woman feels totally responsible for the physical and psychological well-being of her children. She has been conditioned by a lifetime of socialization to feel this way and she does not easily give up or alter such a responsibility. This results in immense guilt and conflict as women attempt to change.

This guilt and conflict is felt by all women and not just Displaced Homemakers. I also do individual, couples and family therapy in a clinic where I see many women who suffer from these same issues regarding identity and self-worth. Some of them may be career women but they also suffer guilt over motherhood. Some women may be on welfare due to poverty but the issues regarding motherhood are there for them as well.

It appears that in the female unconscious is imprinted a model for motherhood that dare not be refuted. This is the model of the mother pictured in the "Madonna with Child." This is the mother who holds her child to her breast and would dare not consider a life for herself. Such a possibility is anathema. I do not think we women understand how powerful this unconscious model of the "Good Mother" is and how potent an influence it has over our lives.

Women today have more options than ever before. We are told that we can have both a career and a family, but internal conflicts as well as external realities tell us that this is not so. We find it very difficult, if not impossible, to deviate from being a traditional mother because the internal and external obstacles are constantly there. As we move toward new ways of being, we come up against social constraints that give way only very slowly. If and when we finally succeed in pushing past them, we meet psychological barriers that must be met and mastered. Conflicts between new ways and old ways are bound to cause turmoil as we struggle with ourselves. The old ways of being die hard, but as the situation currently stands we are being paralyzed by motherhood and it is making it impossible for us to creatively find new ways of being mothers in a modern world.

I feel deep inside of me a painfully intense need to explore these issues of motherhood for myself and for all women. My purpose in writing this book is to create a new vision of motherhood that will reduce the paralysis that motherhood has held for us in the past. I believe strongly that knowledge is power. Raising consciousness is only the first step. The second and most important step is to look directly into the face of the conflicts we still suffer and acknowledge their source. The changes we seek in ourselves as women will not be easy to come by but the acknowledgment of the obstacles that are still standing in our way is a move forward to opening up new possibilities for authenticity and individuation in women. My study of self-actualized women is still a very important endeavor of mine but it now will have to be delayed. For it has suddenly occurred to me that if we women wish to be truly self-actualized, to fully utilize our potential, a new vision of motherhood will be a necessary prerequisite. Hopefully, this book will help pave the road to that goal.

◆ 1 ◆

Where Have All The Mothers Gone?

In the 1980's women have returned to the work force en masse. They have done so for a number of reasons. The high divorce rate and the average age of widowhood (age fifty-six) have shown women that they must be financially capable of taking care of themselves because relationships to men can no longer be counted on to last a woman's full life cycle (77.2 years). Also, the economic realities of today make it virtually impossible for many of those women who are married to live on one income alone. Women have returned to work for the additional reason that working is a source of self-fulfillment that gives them a feeling of achievement. There is an inherent need in all of us to use our potentialities, namely our abilities and dispositions. The actualization of these potentialities is the end result in the process of growth. Consequently, there is no need to wonder where all the mothers have gone. They have gone to work—some because of pure desire but many due to necessity. Leaving their families and returning to the work force has been a source of guilt for most women because this behavior goes against traditional roles.

I can really understand women's guilt about pursuing careers because I also suffer from it. I grew up in a middle class family in the 1950's. My mother never worked outside of the home following her marriage to my father, and she was quite proud of the fact that her daughter seldom had to return to an empty house. The lady down the street did work and my mother and her friends thought her behavior to be quite shocking. I heard their whispering disapproval and thanked my lucky stars that I didn't have a working mother. I was fortunate because I could come home and shout "Hey, mom, I'm home!" and there would be an answer.

As liberated as I have become and as much as I advocate careers for women as fundamental to their development of a self, I still suffer pangs of guilt that I am not home full-time with my children. Men don't have the same guilt and never have. Why is it so difficult for us as women to assert our rights to have a self-identity outside of our motherhood role? Why is it that in the 1980's women are still struggling with this issue? Intellectually we know that we cannot rely on motherhood to give us a sense of self-identity. We know that for our own economic survival we need to become financially independent. We see the reality that women can no longer depend on others to take care of them. We see all these things but still something inside ourselves resists. The old ways of living are still in us internally, and they influence our behavior long after we know that we must live in new ways if we wish to become fully functioning adults in the world.

The pioneering work of Dorothy Dinnerstein and Nancy Chodorow has vastly contributed to our understanding of why women are still struggling with this conflict around motherhood. They believe that there are important psychological repercussions to the fact that only women mother and the fact that it is a woman who is our first primary attachment. Our early development as young girls has set the stage for our reluctance to change. It is important for women to understand what is going on inside them.

The work of Lillian Rubin has been invaluable in helping me comprehend the consequences of the fact that it is a woman who is almost always the primary caretaker in infancy and the developmental repercussion this produces. What happens for us as young girls growing up is that we come to define ourselves by affirming our original connection with mother. Because we are the same gender, it is harder for us to separate from our mother than it is for a boy. In order for a boy to establish his maleness, he must renounce his connection with his mother and seek a deeper identification and attachment with his father. The boy child must repress his identification and attachment to mother, and in order to protect himself from the pain that this repression causes for him, he builds a set of defenses that he will use for the rest of his life. He develops ego boundaries that are fixed and firm—barriers that rigidly separate self from other.[1]

In contrast to boys, girls have a whole different set of obstacles to overcome in the process of developing an independent sense of self. Because there are no obvious differences between a girl and her mother, the establishment of gender identity is easier. The problem of separating and of defining and experiencing self as autonomous is harder for the girl than for the boy.

In the case of girls, the formation of gender identity requires no break with the past. Since she need not displace the internalized representation of the loved mother she has no need to build defenses against feeling and attachment. She has no need for rigid boundaries like those the boy develops as a means of protecting and maintaining those defenses. As a result she develops ego boundaries that are more permeable than the boy's. This fact explains why women have such empathic capacities. A girl never has to separate herself as completely and irrevocably as does a boy. Consequently, her sense of self is never as separate as his and she experiences herself as more continuous with another. The maintenance of close personal connections will continue to be one of life's essential themes for her throughout life. As a result she develops empathy, the capacity for participating in another's inner life and of sensing another person's emotional state almost as if it were her own.[2]

For a woman there is little motivation to establish a separate self as there is for a man. Since she has no reason to barricade herself against the experience of her dependency, no reason to retreat in fear from her vulnerability, relationships seem to hold a promise that connection with another can be trusted and sustained. The problem here is that this promise of attachment is so powerfully seductive for a woman that it draws her dangerously close to violating the boundaries of self. Her preoccupation with connection sometimes feels as necessary as the very air she breathes. This also is the need that motivates the urge to motherhood. It is this same need for attachment and connection that explains why women so consistently have close and intimate friendships with each other.[3]

When women in the 1980's leave home to go out to work they have difficulties in leaving children behind. Fathers work; mothers "mother" even when they also work. Personal connections are extremely important to the woman and she will only reluctantly give up her primacy in relation to the children. For whatever the difficulties in mothering a child, whatever costs to her professionally, there are important gains. What she gains is the intimate connection, the sure knowledge that, whatever else happens, this bond is a permanent one, the sense of power that comes with knowing that she has indelibly marked another's life.[4]

And so the cult of motherhood grows reinforced by the psychological theories about the centrality of the mother-infant bond. Fathers may have been brought into a more active involvement in child raising but it is still the mother-infant bond that gets all the attention. We are only now beginning to ask what the cost of this arrangement is to all of us.

I am beginning to understand why change is so difficult for us as people. Because we have all been raised by mothers, men and women develop distinctly different internal psychic structures and therefore different ways of defining and maintaining a self. Even as we fight the old ideology we struggle with our own psychology.

We may understand intellectually why the woman in the newspaper article did not have custody of her children but our expectations about mothers and motherhood are slow to give way. And in those cases where a divorced mother willingly gives up custody to a father, neither she nor we are wholly comfortable with the choice. She may have a hundred sound reasons for making that decision but guilt usually dogs her inner life and corrodes her peace of mind.[5]

Whether because of guilt, because of their need for connection, or because of some combination of the two, most women don't want to be away from a young child, and the need to do so creates conflict for them. For women, being in this primary position in the life of another is not given up lightly.[6]

The mystique of motherhood is so firmly entrenched in our consciousness that most of us still believe it is damaging to a small child to be cared for by anyone but a mother. Research has proven that this is not so. Psychologists now say that giving up one's life for the sake of children is not healthy mothering. The result of doing so is that children come to believe that they are the center of the universe. They grow up believing that the world owes them a living and are consequently unprepared to deal with the colder realities of life.

Having mothers be the primary caretakers of children has damaging effects that have never been considered before. (These effects will be thoroughly discussed in a later chapter.) Research and clinical evidence supports a new definition of a healthy mother. A healthy mother, as now defined, is one who is a person in her own right. She has established her own identity and doesn't need to use her children to rescue her from a faltering sense of meaninglessness. Her self-definition is not restricted to motherhood and her success in life is not measured by raising a "quality child" that will establish and enhance her value as a person. Therefore, this type of mother is able to allow her children the freedom to be their own unique selves.

This new vision of what it is to be a healthy mother runs against all we have been taught. We may believe it intellectually but it is difficult to accept internally. It is hard to move past this conflict, but doing so is necessary if we are ever to have a world where equality between the sexes exists and both women and men are given an opportunity to fulfill their full human potential.

I believe that by exposing the conflicts involved in the motherhood issue we will come to an understanding of what obstacles we have to overcome on the road to self-actualization. It is important to explore what brought about the creation of the motherhood myth and why it has continued unchallenged. Furthermore, it is crucial to fully comprehend the costs to the development of men, women and children that maintaining this myth involves. Perhaps knowing the price we are paying as a species will give all of us the courage to move beyond our conflicts and forge new frontiers for humankind. Hopefully, we will no longer need to feel guilt, fear, or anxiety when we ask each other where all the mothers have gone because fathers will have claimed their rightful place as co-parents alongside mothers, and children of the future will be more whole and integrated individuals as a result.

◆ 2 ◆

Some History

In doing my research on motherhood I was surprised to discover that motherhood as we know it today is a new institution and is the product of an affluent society. Jessie Bernard states: "In most of human history and in most parts of the world even today, adult able-bodied women have been, and still are, too valuable in their productive capacity to be spared for the exclusive care of children. They have been necessary for tilling the fields or fishing or gathering. In a study of six cultures around the world, including our own, for example, a team of anthropologists and psychologists found only one culture following our model."[7]

In some cultures, the mother works in the fields while the infant is cared for by older siblings. A mother's work load is so heavy in some societies that she trains the children to share it with her as soon as they are able. Bernard reports that the Rajputs of India turn small children and young infants over to the care of an older girl to look after while the mother is busy working. Old men may also help in baby tending. If the child is a boy, as soon as he is able to walk he is turned over to the men—fathers, uncles or grandfathers. Caretaking among the villagers of Taira, Okinawa is shared by all the family

14

relatives. The Mixterans of Mexico transfer the primary caretaking responsibilities from the mother to the siblings about one year after weaning. Among the Alors, since women are primarily responsible for garden work and the subsistence economy, mothers return to regular field work ten days to two weeks after the birth of the child. The infant is left at home in the care of kin, for example the father, an older sibling of either sex, or a grandmother whose field labor is less effective or necessary than that of a younger woman.[8]

In our own society today, parents generally discourage older siblings from assuming responsibility for infants on the grounds that the older child will be irresponsible and that it would also be imposing unduly on him or her. It is thought to be too trying for an older child to face the baby's antisocial behavior and maintain reasonable control over it.[9]

According to Jessie Bernard, the way we institutionalized motherhood in our society—assigning sole responsibility for child care to the mother, cutting her off from the easy help of others in an isolated household, requiring round-the-clock tender, loving care, and making such care her exclusive activity—is not only new and unique, but not even a good way for either women or for children. It may, in fact, be the worst. It is as though we have selected the worst features of all the ways motherhood is structured around the world and combined them to produce our current design.[10]

I found it very interesting to note that the research teams mentioned earlier found that women in cultures where they were given the heaviest load of child care were more changeable in expressing warmth than those in other cultures and more likely to have hostilities not related to the behavior of the children. In fact, the greater the burden of child care assigned to these mothers, the less likely they were to be able to supply the warm care infants require. Maternal warmth was more likely to occur when there was a grandmother present to spell the mother off. Maternal instability decreased when additional caretakers eased the mother's burden and when there were relatively few children requiring her care.[11]

The two requirements that we build into the role of mother are full-time care of children and sole responsibility for them. Bernard sees these as incompatible with one another and even mutually exclusive. It is sobering to note that in our society we seem to maximize this contradiction in the role so that mothers here have a significantly heavier burden (or joy) of baby care than the mothers in any other society.[12]

The isolated home is also a new phenomenon. The privacy of the home originated as a form of protective isolation, but what it was guarding against changed with time. In the fifteenth century it was protection against the evils of communal festivities. In the eighteenth century, the family began to hold society at a distance and was meant to "keep the world at bay." In the nineteenth century the cloistering of the home was a protection against the evils of industrialization and urbanization. The industrial revolution created a male-oriented civilization in which a dog-eat-dog philosophy prevailed and an extremely rugged individualism was needed. There had to be someplace where relief was possible, and that was the home. It became the woman's role to supply "the healing balm to the victors as well as to the victims of the cruel outside world."[13]

Thus the isolated home became a protection from the outside world and it was the mother's responsibility to maintain the home as a sanctuary. In order for mother to perform her sheltering and protective function she had to be protected from the outside world. It was the man's responsibility to guard the woman from the harsh world so that she could create a haven for him to return to. "A loving woman's world lies within the four walls of her own home; and it is only through her husband that she is in any electric communication with the world beyond. Protected, sheltered, isolated, safe within the walls of their gardens, women as mothers became the repositories of all human virtues. It was the mother who made of home a school of virtue."[14]

This attitude led to an increasing idealization of mothers. They were defined as loving, gentle, tender, self-sacrificing, devoted, limited in interests to creating a haven for their families. "Mothers have been honored from time in memoriam, assessed above rubies in value, as the Proverbial woman was, or as the Roman matron was, or the chatelaine of a medieval castle might be. But the mother adored for her self-abnegation, her altruistic surrender, even for her self-immolation, was a nineteenth century Victorian creation. This image reached its heyday at the turn of the century and has lingered on until yesterday."[15]

Even today we see debates about the place of women. The image of the Victorian mother still lurks behind the battle cry "Woman's place is in the home." It has retained a tenacious hold on our minds long after the environment that created and supported it has disappeared.[16]

This concept of motherhood was not authentic—it was more of a fantasy and has led to extreme guilt as women try to achieve it. We set impossibly high standards, and consequently our way of institutionalizing motherhood breeds guilt into every fabric of a woman's character. She blames herself for every deviation from the model. Women are constantly assessing their performances in terms of some ideal standard. Women report: "We often feel guilty, because we think our own inadequacies are the cause of our unhappiness. We rarely question whether the roles we have are realizable." Thus women punish themselves, for "the chief punisher of most deviating mothers is their own conscience. They blame themselves for anything and everything that goes wrong. They are always apologizing for something they have done or not done. The only way some mothers can assuage their guilt is by constant dedication to the child."[17]

It is obvious from our continuing struggle with the motherhood issue that this "Victorian mother" is still alive and well today. She is the dutiful wife and mother who creates in the home a sanctuary for all the higher virtues. There appears to be almost a desperate need for the preservation of such motherliness. "Secure, unthreatened, mother could be, like royalty, above the battle and hence available for the care and nurturance of those hurt and wounded outside its walls as well as those entrusted to her care within them. She could supply solace for the defeated. She could be altruistic because she was not in the fray. She could make the slings and arrows of outrageous fortune in the outside world tolerable. She could be tender and humane. Could she be if she were in the fray herself? If she were an active participant in that harsh competitive outside world? Clearly she could not."[18]

The "Victorian Mother" image is another reason that women are not moving ahead in the world and why they remain paralyzed by their motherhood role. The virtues prescribed for mothers are no more natural for women than for men. Relatively few women achieve all the virtues prescribed for them as mothers but almost all believe they should. They work hard at it and they feel guilty if or when they fail. "If all the people in the mother's world assume and act as if she were going to be self-sacrificing, as though she is going to behave in the interests of others, it becomes all but impossible to act any other way; there is no room for maneuver; the tether is short. Motherhood shapes women, however recalcitrant the material may sometimes be. Whatever materials women bring to motherhood, most do develop the cherishing qualities associated with the role. It is not so much biology as role that was the basis of a woman's virtues."[19]

It appears to me that it is not just the role and that it is not just the fact that all of us were raised by mothers. There appears to be something even more primitive going on in our unconscious that is working to reinforce the nurturing and protective functions of mothers. There seems to be a deep-seated need in all of us to have somewhere, somehow, people who were uncontaminated by the dog-eat-dog practices of capitalism, by the rugged individualism that rewarded the most ruthless and punished the gentle. The conception of the role of mother embodied in this Victorian model produced such healing people. It acted as a defense against the intolerable ambiance that a new industrial-urban society was creating. A study of pre-historic as well as historic remains shows how primordial this assignment of the nurturant and protective function to mothers has been. Since the beginning of time we seemed to have a need for a "Great Mother Goddess" to take care of us. This

"Great Mother" archetype represented not only fertility but also "the sheltering, protecting, and nourishing elementary character."[20]

It is important for us to look at the influence the "Great Mother" archetype has had in perpetuating our motherhood role. It will give us some additional understanding as to why breaking free from this role has been so very difficult.

♦ 3 ♦

The Good Mother Goddess

Mothers have held a special place in all of our lives since the beginning of time. Joseph Campbell, tracing the universality of the Great Mother image from pre-history onward to the present time, asserts that "there can be no doubt that in the very earliest ages of human history the magical force and wonder of the female was no less a marvel than the universe itself; and this gave to woman a prodigious power, which it has been one of the chief concerns of the masculine part of the population to break, control and employ to its own ends." Campbell associates the glorification of hunting over agriculture, and the disappearance of female figurines at the end of the Aurignacian period (c. 30,000 B.C.), with the rise of the male self-assertion against the elemental power of women.[21]

It appears that a "dark" or "negative" aspect of the Great Mother was present from the beginning, insepara-ble from her benign, life-giving aspect. And as death, violence, bloodshed, and destructive power were always there, the potentially "evil" half of the Mother's profile, which once completely split off, would become separate-ly personified as the fanged blood-goddess Kali, the kill-er-mother Medea, the lewd and malign witch, the "castrating" wife or mother.[22]

Woman, with her inexplicable nature and unaccountable attributes and functions, such as menstruation, pregnancy, childbirth and lactation, has been a mysterious person, calling forth a numinous reaction and evaluation, permeated with religious sentiments, rendering her at once sacred and taboo. Anthropological studies point to the many archaic cultures whose cults include a Great Mother with negative aspects of the female.[23]

When analytical psychology speaks of the primordial image or archetype of the Great Mother, it is referring not to any concrete image existing in space and time, but to an inward image at work in the human psyche. The symbolic expression of the psychic phenomenon is to be found in the figures of the Great Goddess represented in the myths and artistic creations of mankind.[24]

The term archetype is generally associated with the psychological theories developed by Carl G. Jung. For Jung, archetypes are primordial images, "structures of the collective unconscious." Jung believes that, in addition to our immediate consciousness which is of a thoroughly personal nature and which we believe to be the only empirical psyche, there exists a second psychic system of a collective universal, of an impersonal nature which is identical in all individuals. This collective unconscious does not develop individually but is inherited. It consists of pre-existent forms, the archetypes, which can only become conscious secondarily and which give definite form to psychic content.

The dynamic, the effect of the archetype, is manifested in energetic processes within the psyche, processes that take place both in the unconscious and between the unconscious and consciousness. "This effect appears, for example, in positive and negative emotions, in fascinations and projections, and also in anxiety, in manic and depressive states, and in the feeling that the ego is being overpowered. Every mood that takes hold of the entire personality is an expression of the dynamic effect of an archetype, regardless whether this effect is accepted or rejected by the human consciousness, whether it remains unconscious or grips the consciousness." The archetype is manifested principally in the fact that it determines human behavior unconsciously but in accordance with laws and independently of the experience of the individual. Furthermore, this dynamic component of the unconscious has a compelling character for the individual who is directed by it, and it is always accompanied by a strong emotional component.[25]

I have personally felt the influence of this "Good Mother" archetype in my own life. There is an intense fear deep inside me that comes rushing to consciousness whenever I deviate from the Victorian mother model. It is almost as if I'm afraid that the earth will open up and serpents will rise out of the nether world hissing at me for my sins against motherhood. I feel an overwhelming anxiety because I know in the deepest recesses of my being that I have gone against some very primitive instinct that dare not be challenged. Intellectually I know that I have nothing to fear, but my unconscious is not convinced that this is so. There are really no words to explain this experience because it is so deeply embedded in my psyche that mere words are inadequate. Other women have reported the same type of experience. This is what it means to be held captive by an archetype.

Thus the archetype of the "Good Mother" is imprinted in our unconscious and is constantly exerting its influence on all of us. The dynamic action of the archetype extends beyond unconscious instinct and continues to operate as an unconscious will that determines the personality, exerting a decisive influence on the mood, inclination, and tendencies of the personality, and ultimately on its conceptions, intentions, and interests, on consciousness and the specific direction of the mind.[26]

This is a possible explanation for why the "Victorian Mother" continues to exist as an ideal. It corresponds with the archetype of the Good Mother and is reinforced therefore unconsciously. Add to this the fact that we were all raised by women and you have a mind set that is extremely difficult to alter.

The term Great Mother, as a partial aspect of the Archetypal Feminine, is a late abstraction, presupposing a highly developed speculative consciousness. It is only relatively late in the history of mankind that we find the Archetypal Feminine designated as the Great Mother. But it was worshiped and portrayed many thousands of years before the appearance of the term. The combination of the words "mother" and "great" is a combination not of concepts but of emotionally colored symbols. "Mother" in this connection does not refer merely to a relationship of filiation but also to a complex psychic situation of the ego, and similarly the term "Great" expresses the symbolic character of superiority that the archetypal figure possesses in comparison with everything human and with created nature in general.[27]

It is important to know that one of the features of the primordial archetype is that it combines positive and negative attributes. Neumann explains that this union of opposites in the primordial archetype is characteristic of the original situation of the unconscious. Early man experienced this paradoxical simultaneity of good and evil, friendly and terrible, in the godhead as a unity, while as consciousness developed, the good goddess and the bad goddess usually came to be worshiped as different beings.[28]

The primordial archetype belongs to a consciousness and an ego that are still incapable of differentiation. The more contradictions that are combined in it, the more confounding and overwhelming are its actions and manifestations. Because so many contradictory motifs and symbols are joined in the archetype, its nature is paradoxical: it can be neither visualized nor represented.[29]

Early man—like the child—perceives the world "mythologically." That is, he experiences the world predominantly by forming archetypal images that he projects upon it. The child, for example, first experiences in his mother the archetype of the Great Mother, that is, the reality of an all-powerful numinous woman, on whom he is dependent in all things, and not the objective reality of his personal mother, this particular historical woman which his mother becomes for him later when his ego and consciousness are more developed.[30]

The negative component of the Great Mother is the "Terrible Mother." Maria Herrera-Sobek calls this the "Treacherous Woman Archetype." She states: "The symbolism of the Terrible Mother draws its images predominantly from the inside; that is to say, the negative elementary character of the Feminine expresses itself in fantastic and chimerical images that do not originate in the outside world. The reason for this is that the Terrible Female is a symbol for the unconscious. And the dark side of the Terrible Mother takes the form of monsters, whether in Egypt or India, Mexico or Etruria, Bali or Rome. In the myths and tales of all peoples, ages, and countries—and even in the nightmares of our own nights—witches and vampires, ghouls and specters, assail us, all terrifyingly alike."[31]

Primitive men feared women, for women were powerful and mysterious beings capable of giving life. Archaic cultures attributed magical powers to females, powers that were incomprehensible to men. Of particular fear to ancient men were the physiological and biological functions of women. Numerous rites and taboos are related to the onset and recurrence of the menstrual cycle, and, even surprisingly, many myths concern the "vagina dentata" which devours men.[32]

Similarly, the destructive side of the feminine, the destructive and deathly womb, appears most frequently in the archetypal form of a mouth bristling with teeth. This motif of the vagina dentata is most distinct in the mythology of the North American Indians. In the mythology of other Indian tribes a meat-eating fish inhabits the vagina of the Terrible Mother: the hero is the man who overcomes the Terrible Mother, breaks the teeth out of her vagina, and so makes her into a woman.[33]

It is important to remind ourselves that even today in our own culture men's identity is based on not being female, a sense that is ultimately rooted in the early separation experiences of infancy. (This developmental process was discussed in Chapter 1.) Feminism threatens this often painfully achieved sense of self and threatens, unconsciously, to throw men into the power of the loved and feared mother. Men identify with the power of the father as a means of repressing the mother (female) inside them, and this results in an unconscious need to keep adult women "in their place" and often in a conscious contempt for them.[34]

If it is true that there are both positive and negative

aspects of the Great Mother, it is understandable that our unconscious could motivate us to isolate women in their homes, place them on a pedestal and keep them "acting out" the qualities of the Good Mother archetype so as to defend against the frightening possibility that women, unrestrained, would turn into the Terrible Mother that we so greatly fear.

Dorothy Dinnerstein gives us some additional insight into the cause of our species' fundamental ambivalence toward its female members. That early mother is a source like nature, a source of ultimate distress as well as ultimate joy. "Like nature, she is both nourishing and disappointing, both alluring and threatening, both comforting and unreliable. The mother, then, like nature, which sends blizzards and locusts as well as sunshine and strawberries, is perceived as capricious, sometimes actively malevolent. She is the source of food, warmth and comfort; but the baby, no matter how well cared for, suffers from some hunger or cold, some aches and pains, some discomfort and some loneliness or boredom; and how is it to know that she is not the source of these too?"[35]

Consequently, the woman is inevitably forced into the dual role of indispensable quasi-human supporter and deadly quasi-human enemy of the human self. Mother is both "Good" and "Terrible." Therefore, it is not surprising to me that both men and women would wish to see forever repressed the negative qualities of the Great Mother and to see expressed in the world only the good qualities. That would explain why consciously and unconsciously it is important to keep women in their place. It is understandable why the Victorian Mother lives on despite feminists' efforts to help women gain power and to become authentic fully-functioning adults.

The following myth is an excellent illustration of this point:

> There is a Persian myth of the creation of the world which precedes the biblical one. In that myth a woman creates the world, and she creates it by the act of natural creativity which is hers and which cannot be duplicated by men. She gives birth to a great number of sons. The sons, greatly puzzled by this act which they cannot duplicate, become frightened. They think, "Who can tell us, that if she can give life, she cannot also take life?" And so, because of their fear of this mysterious ability of woman, and of its reversible possibility, they kill her.[36]

We can kill the woman either literally or more symbolically, by limiting her to a role that limits her potential to be a fully-functioning adult. But we pay a heavy price when we do so. It is important to evaluate the cost to men, women and children alike of relegating women to the role of the "Good Mother Goddess."

♦ 4 ♦

The Silent Disease of Momism

The old belief that a good mother should give her life for her child is now considered by psychologists as poor mothering. Such a mother lacks her own stable identity and this can lead to neurosis. Neurosis emerges in situations where unresolved conflict or deep-rooted uncertainty (especially if it is about one's own self) causes considerable anxiety, tension and unhappiness. As a consequence, the person engages in excessive defense tactics. These tactics have the potential of severely hurting and curtailing the happiness of others, especially if those others are dependent on the neurotic individual.

This neurotic situation all too often applies to the mother-child relationship. Hans Sebald calls this a "Momistic situation." Such a mother tends to suffer profound conflict and discontent concerning her place in life. Her relentless search for self-meaning causes her to have doubts about whether the wife-mother role and the resultant activities associated with it are really meant for her. Often she suffers deep disappointment and frustrations about being limited to the wife-mother role. These emotional dynamics may be out of her conscious awareness; rather, they are unconscious processes.[37]

Because of these doubts and frustrations, the mother

seeks compensation through trying to become a "perfect" mother and in the process uses her child as an indication of her success. As a result, the child acquires deep anxieties and uncertainties about his basic self-worth, and this undermines his mental health. (The masculine generic is used for writing purposes and is meant to include both males and females.) Commonly understood standards of mental health include a person's ability to care for himself and others and to engage in productive work. This implies and requires the ability to make decisions that a mature person should not expect others to make for him. This is the more characteristic defect of the Momistically impaired person: he is incapable of making his own decisions and becomes extremely dependent. Consequently, the impaired person tends to engage in irresponsible behavior due to the fact that the "gyroscope" of judgment and guidance is not within him but outside of him, making this person an easy prey of persuasion and indoctrination. If these forces of influence are irresponsible, the emotionally undeveloped individual will follow suit and act irresponsibly, perhaps even cruelly, and without thought for the consequences.[38] The popularity of cults among young people is an example of this.

The dependency neurosis of the mother becomes as powerful as an addiction, making the child's loyalty and obedience the substance of her craving. The mother thereby succeeds in getting the child addicted to her. Such sick dependency exhibits all the symptoms of drug addiction: the need for a regular "fix," the tolerance level, the withdrawal symptoms, the immaturity growing out of exclusively and compulsively adhering to the one avenue of seeking ways to overcome problems and satisfy security needs.[39]

Such people are said to have a "dependent personality disorder" and I see them frequently in my practice. A person with a dependent personality allows others to assume responsibility for major areas of his life because of a lack of self-confidence and an inability to function independently. This individual subordinates his own needs to those of others on whom he is dependent in order to avoid any possibility of having to be self-reliant.

The development of this dependency begins in childhood and is the result of failure to separate from the mother. Such a child bears the effects of Momism in a latent and rather invisible way. "At the core of the Momistically induced pathology lies the child's—and later (and more obviously) the adult's—inability to achieve a normal degree of self-reliance, make his own decisions, form independent opinions, acquire self-confidence, and engage in responsible behavior." This type of emotionally crippled child has the appearance of a well-behaved and pliable child. But when he grows older and demands are made of him, the pathological condition becomes obvious. The young adult has retained the emotions, attitudes and behavior patterns of a child. Often, profound anxiety accompanies this immaturity, and a consuming preoccupation develops to be accepted and loved by others. What has caused this problem is that a deeply troubled mother has imposed her problems on the child and attempted to obtain compensation and alleviation through him.[40]

One wonders why the negative aspects of motherhood have never been thoroughly examined and exposed. I heartily agree with Sebald that this is probably due to the fact that Motherhood has been a hallowed and sacred tradition in American life, safeguarded by taboos against attack. Motherhood has always been regarded as something that cannot possibly go awry. Thus no one has wanted to investigate the status of mother and her psychological transactions. Another reason we have done little investigation into this issue is due to the fact that it has been only recently that the phenomenon of Momism has started to spread and become a noticeable problem.[41]

There are several reasons that Momism leads to pathology. One technique that a mother employs throughout her child-rearing activities consists of conditional love. She tries to manipulate the child by extending acceptance and love on a conditional basis. A typical mom would not say "I don't like (or love) what you are doing" but, instead, "Mother won't love you if you do that." This approach provides a most powerful and usually very successful lever to make the child obedient and malleable to the wishes and demands of the parent.[42]

This technique only works when the child is first made to believe that mother's love is the most important thing in his life, without which he would be lost and unhappy. So profoundly can a child be conditioned by this emotional premise that he will look upon his mother's love as the ultimate source of security. I used the conditional love approach with my own children because my mother used it on me and probably her mother used it on her. It was only after I had taken some child psychology courses that I learned how damaging such a technique can be on a child. I wasn't intentionally trying to harm my children. It was just that I simply didn't know any better.

Another reason that Momism leads to pathology is that oftentimes mothers gain their sense of identity from being mothers. Thus her value as mother depended entirely on the quality of the child. Moreover, her total human self-worth became contingent on the outcome of her parenthood. A mother who perceived her self-worth in such a manner would energetically pursue to make sure that the "quality child" would establish and enhance her value. If a woman has no other source of power she will live vicariously through her children. If they succeed, then so does she. The child is the product which becomes the mother's means to attaining a solution to the anxieties that stem from her own unfulfilled needs, or from unsuccessful attempts at meeting such needs.

What had happened was that many young mothers were convinced that child-raising was the only major function left in their marriage and family life, and that it was the only alternative to an outside career. Thus mothers entered the project of child-raising with zeal and determination and set about to produce "quality."[43]

I was one of those mothers who didn't believe that a career was an option for me. As I already mentioned, I was raised to believe that working mothers were somehow suspect. I was very frustrated because I had no outlet for my talents and abilities except through my children. If they didn't make the top reading group in first grade, then I saw myself as a failure. When I discovered that it would be necessary for my youngest son to repeat first grade, my initial reaction was one of shame. I had done something wrong. How could a child of such an intelligent mother have to repeat first grade? The simple fact that he just needed another year to mature wasn't a sufficient reason. It had to be my fault in some way. My identity as a mother was so involved with my children's successes or failures that I couldn't even see that we were separate people.

If a mother's need is to establish a stable identity, it is therefore an unfortunate person who has to depend on such an anxious individual. The end result is that the person ends up incurring his share of the pathology. "What may have begun as an idealistic enterprise, with the intention of treating the child as an individual whose growth and maturity were to be safeguarded, ends unhappily with career mothering, because this seems to be the only way for the mother to rescue a faltering sense of meaninglessness and identity. In sum, the child becomes an irreplaceable figure, who is needed by the mother so that she can deduce her identity as Mother—which is capitalized to denote the central meaning that this status and activity have for her identity and self-definition."[44]

There are many mothers who live vicariously through their children's lives and do not even realize that they are doing so. They may want to pursue a career but their guilt over abandoning their children and not living up to the "Victorian Ideal Mother" is too great. They do not realize the price that their children pay for this, as well as the costs to themselves.

The Breeding Ground for Momism

The current American scene is a breeding ground for "Momism." The traditional household was not limited to "nuclear" members but included grandparents, uncles, aunts and cousins. Thus a child was in close association with a number of blood relatives. The family was larger due to parents' having more children. Thus it made for a considerably larger family unit than the typical nuclear family.

Due to the size of the household and the work load of the adults, parents found little opportunity to take time out to consciously and independently counsel and exert influence over their offspring. What happened instead was that the major interaction and process of growing up occurred among the children themselves. Siblings were important sources of fundamental education for each other. Adults were clearly visible in their daily life and work and could be emulated or rejected with near impunity since selectivity was possible among a larger number of men and women. If you didn't get along with your mother you had other adults to go to for support and encouragement.[45]

In today's family the child has no selectivity in models on which he can pattern his attitudes. If the role model is unacceptable to the child, he is stuck. He is trapped in a small and relatively isolated family unit and has limited possibilities to look elsewhere for a consistent adult image. The young child is therefore almost exclusively exposed to the influence of his parents' emotions.

We are beginning to see some changes in family life due to the high divorce rate. When divorced parents marry another partner there is a new family unit. This new family unit is often referred to as a "blended family." There are some distinct advantages to this type of family because there are more people in it. Consequently, if a child has a poor relationship with a father or mother there is the possibility of establishing a more effective relationship with the stepfather or stepmother. Blended families have many of the same qualities that were once typical of extended families. It is somewhat less likely that a child will be exclusively exposed to one parent's immature emotions.

But the fact still remains that in most of today's families, it is still the mother whom the child is primarily exposed to due to the fact that the father has little interaction with the child since he is much less involved with the child-raising process. Consequently, if the mother is not psychologically healthy, the child has no other models of authentic adulthood to turn toward. Philip Slater points out some of the deep-seated problems inherent in the mother's role in the nuclear family. He states:

> In our society the housewife may move about freely, but since she has nowhere to go and is not a part of anything anyway her prison needs no walls. This is in striking contrast to her pre-marital life, if she is a college graduate. In college she is typically embedded in an active group life with constant emotional and intellectual stimulation. College life is in this sense an urban life. Marriage typically eliminates much of this way of life for her, and children deliver the "coup de grace." Her only significant relationship tends to be with her husband, who, however, is absent most of the day. Most of her social and emotional needs must be satisfied by her children, who are hardly adequate to the task. Furthermore, since she is supposed to be molding them into superior beings she cannot lean too heavily upon them for her own needs, although she is sorely tempted to do so. This is, in fact, the most vulnerable point in the whole system. Even if the American housewife were not a rather deprived person, it would be the essence of vanity for anyone to assume that an unformed child could tolerate such massive inputs of one person's personality. In most societies the impact of neurosis and defects in the mother's character is diluted by the presence of many other nurturing agents. In middle-class America the mother tends to be the exclusive daytime adult contact with a mission to create a near perfect being. This means that every maternal quirk, every maternal hang-up, and every

maternal deprivation will be experienced by the child as heavily amplified noise from which there is no respite.[46]

It is too bad that Slater's insights are seriously weakened by his phrase "if she is a college graduate." Just because a woman does not go to college doesn't mean that she is happy with "feminine," passive, hearth-centered goals and has no problems with them. "Motherhood does not only imprison women who are articulate enough to say that they feel jailed. The truth is that the traditional set-up puts all women in an impossible role."[47]

It is not a proof of love to spend every minute of the day with another person. According to Bruno Bettelheim, doing so results in a circular trap. "The more the mother is the only adult contact a child has, the more important that contact becomes. The more a child is the only contact (or purpose) a mother has, the more intense and intrusive her behavior will be."[48]

Today's modern family consists of individuals who relate to each other on the basis of extremely demanding emotions. This reflects psychological incompleteness on the part of each of them and creates the tendency to be "glued" to someone else in order to function and feel alive. They develop "dependent personalities." The result is that people live according to sterile roles, with stifled creativity and rigid, unadaptive personalities, rather than as free and autonomous beings.[49]

The Motherhood Myth

With the advent of industrialization and urbanization, family life began to change over the years, and

mothers acquired more freedom from the age-old tread-
mill of basic menial tasks and they raised their expectations in all sectors of life. They came to look at having
and raising children in a new light. Hans Sebald points
out that there came a greater awareness of the role of
mother. She was no longer simply an auxiliary to the
father. This new status culminated in a myth, an almost
cultic devotion to the new "specialized career" of motherhood. "A profound need had been at work to replenish
with meaningfulness the void created by dwindling away
of the daily survival chores mothers had tended to for
ages. The Myth was the answer to the Need. Young
mothers became mother-entrepreneurs."[50]

Mothers suffered certain frustrations in the process.
They felt an increasing urge to experience tangible results and to produce products. But their work became
less and less concerned with production and they were
compelled to waste a vast amount of time on repetitious
and uninteresting tasks. Thus psychological rewards became rare in the modern household.

The modern housewife lacked the feeling of com-
pleting and producing something. She felt frustrated
within the confines of the modern household. "As an
attempt to assuage this frustration, she may have selected motherhood as a means to regain a modicum of the
sense of production completion. Hence many mothers,
resembling so many determined entrepreneurs, set out
to see the production process of their child's personality
through to the end."[51]

The advent of Women's Liberation did little to
change this. Most young American mothers, in spite of
more liberated visions, were still incarcerated by the
structural legacy of the social order, which always tends
to lag behind ideas and dreams. "Formal as well as infor-

mal social arrangements continued to maintain and reinforce the traditional male and female roles. In other
words, whether they liked it or not, women found that
they continued to be mothers and wives with limited
opportunities. Whatever improvements appeared to be
possible had to be obtained largely within the old structural set-up. And this is where the Myth of Motherhood,
as a presumably blissful, creative, productive career,
helped to dull the edge of disappointment and frustration. The myth served as rationalization and solace at the
same time."[52]

In reality the myth was artificial. "Mothers wallowed
in the aesthetics of it all—natural childbirth and nursing
became maternal musts. Like heavy-bellied ostriches,
they grounded their heads in the sands of motherhood,
only coming up for air to say how utterly happy and
fulfilled they were." Mothers may have been unhappy
but the myth has survived, and even gained momentum.
Sebald, as well as other writers, finds it remarkable that
the Motherhood Myth persisted in the face of tremendous maternal unhappiness and incompetence. Still, the
Cultist devotion has continued, and is still being prac-
ticed.[53] Considering women's socialization and the unconscious influence of the "Great Mother" archetype, I
am personally not surprised that the myth has lived on.

The Causes and Effects of Momism

Americans look to marriage and the family as a
hospitable setting for answering the question, "Who am
I?" This puts a gigantic burden on family life and results
in a new emotional strain on the parent-child relationship. The child has now acquired a unique value. He has

become an emotionally important figure, a different creature from the child of generations past. "Then, he had usually been considered unavoidable—a socialization task undertaken almost coincidentally by blood-related peers and adults—assessed as a usable force in the family's division of labor. Now he has become an end in himself, a self-contained entity, a product soon to be sent on his own way—presumably without hindrance on the part of the parents."[54]

But what often happens is that the child is used by the mother for her own gain. Sebald explains that this is due to the fact that American females (particularly mothers) have come to insist—understandably from their viewpoint as equal persons—on trying to partake of the "glories" of successful work, no matter what the cost. The more pronounced their sense of equality, the greater their desire for "self-realization" and "self-actualization." For many, this was achieved by "producing" a child. The emphasis here is not on the biological process but on the psychological dynamics. "Females wanted to create and achieve like everybody else, and many females invested this drive in child-raising. The child became an object, the main ingredient of the psychological concoction such a mother was going to brew, and through which she would try to establish herself as an achiever. Such an endeavor satisfied her newly acquired success drive, and ultimately provided her with a sense of identity."[55]

It is important to remind ourselves of the fact that mothers are not intentionally trying to harm their children. The problem is that mothers have traditionally had little opportunity to develop their own sense of self-identity. Their sense of self has been derived from their husbands and children. Consequently, the woman's own natural talents and abilities have not had an adequate outlet. This can be very destructive to children because life insists on being lived, and anything that belongs to life which is allowed to lie dormant has to be lived by someone else. "If we do not accept our shadow we force our children to carry the burden of our undeveloped capacities. They may become mediocre scientists or artists because we denied our own talents. They may become doctors, which they are not suited to be, because we failed to use our innate capacity for healing, or inept politicians to fulfill our unlived ambitions."[56]

What is really sad is that Momism has continued to grow almost unabated. The reason for this is well stated by Edward Strecker: "And far from the least of the Mom causes, because it is the fertile soil in which the seeds of Momism grow, is our social system and our way of life. Pretty much everything we do—socially, politically, educationally—glorifies Mom and praises her self-sacrifice and her giving her life for her children."[57]

The real consequence of Momism is that the child becomes psychologically impaired. The child becomes an individual whose center of gravity—whose core or orientation and organization—is not anchored in himself. From this lack of true selfhood arise a number of telling characteristics: (1) inability to make decisions, (2) chronic feelings of inferiority, (3) frequent and easily aroused anxieties, (4) irresponsible actions, and (5) a general parasitism, manifesting unchecked narcissism and immature egocentrism.[58]

Some of the psychological factors that lead women to Momism are described by Hans Sebald. It is very important for us to understand what particular background factors cause women to become mothers who produce "momistically impaired" children. Some of these possible factors are:

1. The formation of a Mom may be influenced by the opportunity of imitating one's mother, who is the Mom type.

2. The opportunity to imitate may have been combined with experiences that generated hostility against males. Sometimes her Momistic ways can be veritable revenge for disadvantages or harm, real or imagined, she has suffered at the hands of one or several males. Possibly her father played the salient role of villain in her young life.

3. An outstanding background feature which may lead to Momistic development is the weak and submissive father. She may have witnessed her mother acting in a domineering and overbearing manner toward her father and consequently came to perceive men as weak and indecisive creatures. As wife and mother, she perpetuated these attitudes and directed them toward her husband and son. Her domination and overprotectiveness gave the child little chance to grow up and become an independent person.

4. The Momistic tendency can possibly be traced to extreme experiences of powerlessness in a girl's life. The young woman may compensate by wielding excessive power—seeking an antidote for her former powerlessness by reigning mightily.

5. Momism may result from having experienced emotional neglect in childhood, so that love and care that were not found in early life are lavished on one's child. In effect, the child is used as a mirror of love, who is not treated as a separate entity endowed with a potential uniqueness. This type of love is not real love; it does not accept the child in his own right. Instead, the mother projects her needs onto the child and addresses herself not to his personality but to the needs of her own personality.

6. A mother may take a turn toward Momism because of a disappointing and impassive husband who does not fulfill her craving for intimacy, sexual and otherwise. Her demands for intimate communication, personal attachment, and affection drive her toward the child, from whom she expects the surrender of his preference for age-appropriate intimacy with his peers. Under the guise of personal dedication and "closeness," she uses the child as a substitute for a non-responsive husband.

7. Momism can also emerge from "reaction formation" which is a complex psychodynamic principle. The mother pretends love and kindness but harbors hostility underneath. The emotions of hatred can be so powerful and frightening to the mother that she must suppress them, since awareness and admission of them would endanger her ego ideal: that is, the way she would like to be. She practices deceit within herself.

8. Other women become Moms because they are in search of a cause, any cause—and it happens that their cause becomes the child. These are the mothers who

flaunt motherhood as a noble devotion and use it as a safe island in an otherwise empty existence. Once again the child is used as a means. The child must fill the void of an otherwise meaningless and purposeless existence of the mother. In the process the child is made to experience excessive feelings of inadequacy and guilt. The child is called upon to provide something that not even God can provide. It is the task of every human being to figure out and determine his own meaning in life.[59]

These are some excellent explanations for the origins of Moms. It is important to note that behind all of these various expressions lurks a mother who is characterized by a typical psychological makeup. Such a mother has the following characteristics: emotional immaturity, lack of the ego strength to draw a boundary between her own ego and the ego of her child, and inability to grant her child emotional and intellectual independence. The method Moms use to accomplish compliance with their dreams and demands is the conditional love technique. They use it because it works. Through it they come closest to achieving satisfaction, alleviation, and compensation for their real or imagined hurt and deprivation.[60]

The statistical incidence of Momism among American mothers is at best an intelligent guess but the suspicion is that it is increasing in rate and number—most probably in direct correlation with the further rise and development of urban-industrial conditions. According to Sebald, more and more case studies reveal that the genesis of neurotic problems can be traced to the neurotic problems of the mother. Investigators have discovered that the causes of the neurotic problems of these mothers are intricately tied to the conditions of urban-industrial living and our emancipated and egalitarian culture. Therefore, it is logical to assume that the further evolving of certain urban-industrial conditions will create greater numbers of neurotic mothers who will create increasing numbers of neurotic offspring. This process has been going on for at least one or two generations.[61]

Momism is not only a psychological problem but also a sociological one. It appears mainly in the American middle class, where urban-industrial factors combine to prepare the ground for Momism. There are a number of social and psychological factors, and a particular interrelationship among them, prevailing in the middle class setting which makes it easy for Momism to flourish.[62]

> These conditions include the psychological peculiarity of the halfway-emancipated mother, the remoteness of the father from the child-raising process, the existence of only one child in the family (or, at most, two children), the "educated" and objectified approach to the mother-child relationship, parents' excessive endorsement of competition as a method for raising a "successful" child, the frequency of the situation in which the mother is a divorcee, and the absence of a "rite of passage" for the growing offspring that could promote his self-definition and independence at and above a certain age. If these social-psychological circumstances are the prime movers in the rise of Momism, then societies that acquire these characteristics will also acquire Momism.[63]

It is my belief that Momism is alive and well and flourishing. As long as women have limited access to fulfilling and well-paying careers and are primarily responsible for child care, and as long as society continues to put a guilt trip on women if they attempt to break away from the "Victorian Mother" image, the conditions which foster Momism will continue to exist. Add to these conditions the fact that almost all of us have been raised by women and the influence of the archetype of the "Good Mother Goddess" and we have a situation that will be very difficult to alter. We will have the incentive to change if and when we become convinced of the damage to all of us that will be the result of holding on to the "status quo."

We have been focusing primarily in this chapter on the harmful effects of Momism on the child, but what are some of the consequences to the mother herself? How is she limited by this Motherhood Myth? Furthermore, why do mothers so readily accept such a limited role for themselves? You would think all women would be fighting tenaciously for social change. A thorough understanding of the price women are paying is imperative to our study.

◆ 5 ◆

Women as Children

Why do women themselves often eagerly accept the limited role that society has put upon them? Emphasis on individuation and expansion of opportunity for self-development of women has increased in recent years partially as a result of the Women's Liberation movement. Public reactions to this have ranged from favor to ambivalence and antagonism. Women are being confronted daily by their own urges to fulfill their potentials and by counter-demands from their families and communities to conform to traditional female roles. Women are also confronted by pressures exerted by the women's movement to recognize a variety of possibilities that females can create for themselves. These pressures are found by more than a few women to be very threatening. To the extent that the source of the threat is perceived as external to themselves, it may often be dealt with by environmental manipulations to reduce the stress.[64]

It is therefore not surprising to psychologist Martha Rogers that such books as *The Total Woman* (Morgan, 1975) and *Fascinating Womanhood* (Andelin, 1974) became popular and rapidly caught the interest of middle-class America. Some of the women attracted by the

47

philosophy espoused by these books may have found relief from anxiety-provoking demands for increased role flexibility. By defining roles more rigidly, anxiety is reduced to a more tolerable level. Andelin's book, in particular, suggests the living out of sex roles in caricature. Andelin makes the following points:

1. The woman's role is to know and to analyze all her husband's needs, to anticipate them, and to adapt herself to them totally.

2. Meeting her own needs is to be done by appealing to her helplessness and her dependency, and through her behaving in a charming, childlike manner.

3. Any separate serious interests other than those rigidly defined as suitable for a wife/mother and not in conflict with any of her husband's expectations are unfeminine and unattractive, as well as threatening to the man's masculinity.[65]

I heartily agree with Rogers that it is reasonable to assume that investing one's energy entirely to assuage the needs of others does not create an ideal situation for getting acquainted with oneself. Becoming more of a child and using tactics of a child in maintaining some control over one's life is not conducive to emotional maturation. Furthermore, rigid adherence to narrowly defined sex roles does serve an anxiety reducing function, as does regression, which is permitted and encouraged by this formula. But if (or when) these calculated manipulations are unsuccessful in bringing about the bliss which is promised (i.e., total security and provision of *raison d'être),* the woman may then be in an even more vulnerable and dysfunctional position and may then resort to a victim or martyr role.[66]

Colette Dowling, in her very popular book *The Cinderella Complex,* agrees with Rogers. She sees the woman who devotes her entire life to keeping her husband straight and her children "protected" as not a saint, but a clinger. Rather than experience the terrors of being cut loose, of having to find and secure her own moorings, she will hang on in the face of unbelievable adversity. If she's really good at it, she doesn't appear to suffer much. She looks on the bright side.[67]

The "Good Woman" does her damnedest to please others. In the process she neglects her own developmental tasks. Developmentally, she has gotten as far as high school. She uses marriage in the "service of regression." "She unconsciously hopes to return, through her relationship with her husband, to an earlier, safer time. Marriage becomes a way of being taken care of and supported . . . a way of acquiring a home instead of making one . . . an opportunity to relieve conflict instead of mastering it."[68]

Involvement in "fascinating womanhood" concepts may represent a regression, or a retreat from having to consider the multiple options of personhood today or relating to others from a basis of self-awareness and understanding. The solution offered in *Fascinating Womanhood* brings only a temporary reprieve from personal or marital distress, and more healthy women find it totally unworkable.[69]

It is not merely the books by Morgan and Andelin that are detrimental to women becoming fully functioning adults. Even the very famous and successful Dr. Joyce Brothers has a word of advice to give new mothers. She states: "It all adds up to offering your husband only your best self. Forgo the luxury of indulging in moods of irritability, discontent, and envy. These are luxuries. It means one more strike against you in your effort to keep the irreplaceable treasure—your husband's romantic love. . . . Your problem is to be sure you remain a woman, just as alluring, feminine and interesting to your husband as before the advent of the child. That, in addition to your responsibilities as a mother, will give you a very, very full-time job."[70]

No woman is capable of doing what Dr. Brothers suggests unless she is super-human. Such a goal is unrealizable and unhealthy as well. With such advice it is no wonder so many women come to counseling seeking treatment for troubled marriages. I see these women frequently in my practice and agree with Rogers that these women oftentimes appear to be out of touch with their own needs and wishes, since they habitually define themselves in terms of their husband's or children's needs or expectations. It is interesting to note that when Rogers worked with couples she oftentimes found that while husbands outwardly and consciously voiced the wish that the wife would become more independent, he simultaneously sabotaged her efforts as well as subtly undermined her confidence. Before any changes could be made in the marriage, it was important for the husband to recognize and appreciate the long-term advantages of relating to a woman who has become her own person. It is my belief that such a woman would be an exciting and challenging partner.

Many of these women who come for therapy verbalize the belief that they are staying in their marriages because there is no other choice, while others rationalize that remaining is a genuine choice, yet continue to feel quite angry toward their spouses (which is a good clue to recognize default, not choice). "The social disapproval of divorce in many families and religious communities may be a factor in her default, but usually overriding this consideration is her terror of the world out there without him. She is not fully convinced in an existential sense that she will survive as a person without him. And she may become quite angry at the therapist for raising questions about her options. However, until she experiences herself as having choices and as actually making decisions she will not finish her anger and complete the therapeutic tasks."[71]

Women's Experience of Powerlessness and Fear

Women are oftentimes afraid to admit the intensity of the anger of being in such a powerless position in their marriages. They use denial as a defense and come to therapy with chronic headaches, nervous stomach, colitis, depression and a host of other ailments that are physical signs of repressed anger. These women are shocked to discover that release of this anger and insight into causes of it often leads to the disappearance of the symptoms.

In working with "Displaced Homemakers" I have found fear of being on one's own to be a primary issue. These women have no definition of self outside of their role as wife. They depended on husbands to take care of them and believe that they cannot survive without them. I spend a lot of my energy working with these women to overcome their fear.

It is my belief that women do not know how to

conquer fear because, when we were afraid as children, we were socialized to retreat to the safety of home and parents. In contrast, men were socialized as young boys to go out into the world and conquer whatever it was that frightened them. Men may be just as afraid as women but they don't allow fear to immobilize them. They act on it while women merely retreat back to safety. A sense of power is the result of confronting fear, and women who are able to move ahead despite being afraid become potent as a result.

Colette Dowling also sees fear as a dominating factor in women's lives. She believes that the first thing that women must come to recognize is the degree to which fear rules their lives. "Women who want to start feeling better about themselves must begin by facing what's going on inside. Women will not become free until they stop being afraid. We will not begin to experience real change in our lives, real emancipation, until we begin the process—almost a de-brainwashing—of working through the anxieties that prevent us from feeling competent and whole."[72]

Women can move beyond fear. There is immense satisfaction for me as I watch "Displaced Homemakers" take positive steps on their own behalf. With a lot of support from each other as well as from myself, they begin to conquer their fears of being alone and discover the glorious benefits to being a person who has the power to be self-defining. With every step these women take they gain the inner strength to take another step forward. In this process they are gaining inner security which is the only security one really has in today's rapidly changing world. Women need to know that they, alone, can survive no matter what blows life deals them.

Facing Our Problems

It is unfortunate but true that there are many women who will not go to therapists because of the traditional suspiciousness felt toward mental health professionals by persons of strong religious leaning. As a result, these women are attracted to courses with theological underpinnings of "total woman" and "fascinating womanhood." Rogers understands their suspicion but sees it as very sad because these women who are incompletely individuated may be potentially more vulnerable to extreme dysfunction through developmental crises such as children leaving home or loss of husband through divorce or death. Old age may be experienced as successive loss of parts of oneself. Such crises may be prevented or partially alleviated by therapy that promotes individuation.[73]

There are psychological costs involved in the traditional housewife role. Distress is experienced by many women when the demands of motherhood cease or diminish and they are faced with premature retirement. Some interesting findings of researchers are as follows:

1. Maternal role loss was found to be a significant factor in precipitating depression among hospitalized women. Those with over-protective or over-involved relationships with their children were particularly vulnerable to depression. Lack of meaningful work involvement appeared also to be a factor. These women did not consider their work important, and when asked what they were most proud of, none mentioned any accomplishment of their own—rather, they were proud of their children.[74]

2. The onset of alcoholism in middle-aged women was frequently associated with the "empty nest syndrome." These women were usually dependent upon their husbands and/or children for their identity and their sense of worth and purpose. They had built their lives around their families and had few interests not directly related to their husbands or children.[75]

3. There were significantly higher psychiatric symptom scores exhibited by women not employed outside the home than by women employed full-time, with part-time employed women occupying an intermediate position. This suggests that the traditional housewife role often has a tragic personal consequence for women. They are forced into premature retirement, and this is sometimes accompanied by anxiety and depression as maternal demands cease or diminish. Unless the degree of commitment to volunteer work approximates that of paid employment, it does not provide the same feelings of self-worth or accomplishment.[76]

Given all the evidence that accepting the Motherhood Myth is detrimental to women, one wonders why women so willingly accept it. There are women who truly love everything about being housewives and mothers. They feel that there is nothing that could possibly give them more satisfaction than motherhood. The attachment and connection to another person that this role provides is powerfully seductive. In Simone de Beauvoir's analysis the problem is to understand why women accept the limitations of this role. She states:

> If men find in women more complicity than the oppressor usually finds in the oppressed, it is because

women, from earliest childhood, are offered more enticing inducements to play the role assigned them. Against the difficult assertion of self, woman is beguiled with a promise of security not offered to the male. She is led to believe that she does not need to create her future through her own actions in the present; her vocation, in the form of marriage and motherhood, will happen to her. If she accepts the feminine role of Other, she denies herself the opportunities of transcendence, but also is safe from its hazards. Her femininity is the mirage that she will be taken care of, not only economically but absolutely. All the elements of woman's situation encourage her to prefer the pleasures of passivity and the repose of definition to the risks and uncertainties of freedom.[77]

It is the woman most avidly seeking transcendence who is often most vulnerable to the religion of love. Denied the transcendence of action and adventure offered to the male, she seeks transcendence by losing herself in a man (or in a child) who represents the essential which she cannot be for herself. Beauvoir is not warning women against love but against love as an absolute, a promise of salvation. "When woman, fully the equal of man, can love in her strength and not in her weakness, love will become for her as for man a source of life and not of mortal danger. To expect salvation from someone other than oneself is the surest and quickest way to lose oneself. Man wants woman to be object; she makes herself object; at that very moment when she does that, she is experiencing a free activity. Therein is her original treason."[78]

The price women pay for accepting the "Motherhood Myth" is high indeed. But women who truly desire to be mothers and take their motherhood seriously but do not want to lose themselves in the process need to answer the crucial question: What do children really need? An exploration of this question is therefore extremely necessary.

♦ 6 ♦

What Do Children Really Need?

In the 1890's mothers were encouraged to respond to every signal that the child emitted. In the 1920's mothers were told to leave the child in peace—to reduce, not to increase their commitment. Both of these recommendations were by experts in child psychology. Experts either worried about the neglected child or they despaired over "the overkissed child."

There has always been confusion about what is really good for children. But the traditional belief in our society, held by many professional psychologists, is that women must stay home with their children, particularly in the early years, in order to be good mothers. This belief was based in part on results of studies of institutionalized children indicating that long-term separation of the child from the mother during the pre-school years may have detrimental effects on the child's subsequent intellectual, social and emotional development. Others have stressed that there are differences between residential care and the briefer, repeated separations characteristic of the non-maternal care experienced by children of working mothers.[79] However, recent reviews by Clair Etaugh indicate that maternal employment per se is not harmful to the child.

Etaugh has done an extensive study of the effects of non-maternal care on children. Her report tells us that several studies have compared the maternal attachment behaviors of children reared at home and of children entering non-maternal care before the age of two. These studies have found highly similar patterns of attachment behavior in the two groups. Other studies have compared attachment reactions to the mother and to the substitute care-giver among children experiencing non-maternal care. These indicate that the child can form an attachment to a stable substitute care-giver that parallels the development of attachment to the mother.[80]

The bulk of evidence indicates that non-maternal care starting in the first two years of life does not impair the child's attachment to the mother. Under favorable circumstances such experience may make it somewhat easier for children to adapt comfortably to unfamiliar social situations requiring a willingness to tolerate some distancing from the mother.[81]

A reasonably cautious conclusion that can be drawn from the available data is that high-quality non-maternal care does not appear to have harmful effects on the pre-school child's maternal attachment, intellectual development, social-emotional behavior, or physical health.[82]

The popular press has tended to perpetuate the belief that non-maternal care is harmful to young children. There is even some evidence of this belief in some popular writings of the 1970's despite research evidence to the contrary. Many of the attacks on day care in the popular press have focused on day care as it typically exists, whereas research on non-maternal care has dealt largely with high-quality day care.[83]

It is my belief that high-quality day care should be a

high national priority. If the first six years of a child's life are as critical as the experts say they are, then our highest national priority should be thinking of new ways to maximize children's development during those years. Putting all this responsibility exclusively on mothers is not the answer.

Cross-cultural studies suggest that adjustment is most facilitated when the child is cared for by many friendly people. Sociologist Nancy Chodorow comments that recent research suggests that children need consistency of care and the ability to relate to a small number of people stably over time. They do not require an exclusive relationship to one person. It is Chodorow's view that exclusive single parenting is bad for mother and child alike. She believes this because mothers in such a setting are liable to overinvest in and overwhelm the relationship. It is her contention that children are better off in situations where love and relationship are not a scarce resource controlled and manipulated by one person only.[84]

There are some specific advantages to women working outside the home. A mother's employment prevents her from exerting continuous power and influence over the child, and hence protects the child from her possibly neurotic tendencies and conflicts. In addition, the child is free to explore other human relationships. He or she learns to adjust to peers and is able to choose among various adult models. As a consequence, the child experiences a richer scope of intellectual and emotional stimulation.[85]

A Healthy Motherhood Script

What do children really need? Hans Sebald believes that children need mothers who follow a wholesome motherhood script. This script must emphasize:

1. Unconditional love, not conditional love. Love based on conditions of compliance is the most vicious tool that moms have and it creates crippling anxieties. Healthy motherhood reaches out and offers unconditional love that supports the child's sense of self-worth.

2. Strong selfhood instead of parasitic needs. The higher the strength of self in a mother, the less self-centered she is. Secure selfhood frees her from making overly selfish demands on others and enables her to help without ulterior motives.

3. Freely chosen motherhood, not the motherhood compulsion that is a product of the Motherhood Myth. What is badly needed is a full awakening to the fact that motherhood is just one alternative among a number of different life-styles. The assumption that having children is the essence of a woman's life is as myopic as it is dangerous. Motherhood as a way of life has been oversold to American women.

4. The child as an end and not as a means. Mom fails to visualize the uniqueness of the child and constantly compares him with others. This comparison is extended to careers generally, and she feels that for the sake of motherhood she has bypassed other worthwhile careers. This creates a feeling of deprivation in her, a need to compensate for it, and the tendency to use the child as a

success symbol. The healthy script must discourage this. Motherhood either comes from the heart, and it is truly a loving experience, or the role should not be played at all.

5. Discipline, not overindulgence. While the overindulgent mother pampers an egocentric and selfish personality, the mother who puts a normal emphasis on discipline will help her child grow up to be a responsible and well-oriented human being.

6. Care and concern, not overprotection. The child must have the benefit of feeling cared for and knowing he can approach the parent with his problems. Otherwise he will feel lonely, rejected and insecure. On the other hand, overprotection is a perversion of care. It exceeds normal needs for protection, it denies the child exploration of reality on his own, and it prevents him from becoming a self-reliant and mature individual.

7. Guidance, not domination. Domination does not allow the unfolding of the child's maturity and sense of responsibility. He gets accustomed to accept outside agents as authority for each and every action, and does not develop a sense of evaluation based on his personal judgment and knowledge. On the other hand, normal guidance and instruction are a must for the child's welfare. Without such attention, he will not develop a sane sense for assessing reality.

8. Knowledge and information, not pseudo-intellectualism. The responsible mother is eager to learn to be a good parent and is open to professional advice and counseling. The pseudo-intellectual mother tries to impress. Her goal (although mostly unconscious) is to en-

slave the child—and everybody else who falls for her facade of learnedness. An expert on relatively insignificant details, she has lost sight of basic purposes of the child-rearing process, such as true maturity for the child. She persuades the child to learn intellectual trivia, but fails to give him the emotional strength to integrate the details and apply them to some fruitful goal.[86]

A Healthy Fatherhood Script

How do fathers fit into this act of parenting? Sebald also has a script for the father and believes that while the mother-turned-mom is guilty of acts of commission, the father in the Momistic situation is guilty of acts of omission. The father does nothing to balance the scales of child nurturing. Being so busy elsewhere, fathers refuse to share their lives with their own sons and indirectly teach these boys to retreat from their responsibilities. The masculine script, as we know it today, omits the necessary encouragement for the male to be a child-raiser, as demonstrated by the fact that our vocabulary provides us with the word "mothering" but not "fathering" for the job of bringing up the child.[87A]

Sebald offers some specific recommendations for reshaping the father's script to bring about a more balanced and equitable performance of the parental function. He believes that the creative and mom-resistant paternal role can be safeguarded by:

1. Genuine willingness to extend fathering. Many males have ambivalent, if not aversive, feelings about fathering, yet they go ahead with it. Just as there is a

Motherhood Myth there is an equivalent, though less emphatic, Fatherhood Myth. It propels the male toward the biological act of fathering without being fully willing to accept the responsibilities to continue with social fathering. By excluding ambivalent and unwilling males from fatherhood, a giant step toward the improvement of child-raising could be made. Obviously, this suggestion will run into the same difficulty as the attack on indiscriminate motherhood by stirring up the old excuse and defensiveness about "parenthood as a natural right for anybody." This "free choice" of the father script should be curbed (at least by educational means) by setting a different emotional tenor for fatherhood by emphasizing (and enforcing) the everyday chores and responsibilities to be shared with the mother.

2. The flexible father script. The new script should allow respectability in a man's choosing to be a "homebody" and wanting to take care of a household and the child-raising. The choice of being a "house-husband" should not have derogatory connotations.

3. The diffused breadwinner role. Occupational career functions should be distributed according to likes and proficiencies. The masculine role is not to be seen as diminished because the wife pursues a career and shares in the breadwinning for the family.

4. Active involvement in home chores. Balanced child-raising calls for balanced investment of time and energy between the mother and father. It is important for the child to see different personalities at work and to escape the overbearing influence of one and the same

person, thereby possibly avoiding the harm that could come to him through overexposure to a disturbed parent.

5. Educational preparation for the father script. The pre-maternal courses for young wives, which have been encouraged in some communities, should be redefined and include men as well. Such pre-parental education should focus equally on men and women and help bring out their potential for raising their children. Preparatory courses should introduce them to various aspects connected with bringing up the child: rudimentary child psychology, physical care and health, hygiene, nutrition, clothes, budgeting, shopping, etc.

6. The expanded male script. In order to balance the female influence, males must expand their occupational interest into careers hitherto relatively shunned by males, especially as they apply to teaching in nurseries, kindergartens, and elementary schools.

7. Reshaping cultural images. None of the above suggestions can be implemented without considering the traditional definitions of masculinity and femininity. These definitions must be loosened and rewritten. Interaction between the parents and between the parents and their children must proceed on a more individualistic (rather than culturally ossified) basis.[87B]

The proposed modifications of the father's script aim at bringing into our vocabulary the word "fathering" as representing a definite and mandatory aspect of parenthood. All of us would benefit from such changes in parenting. I believe that what is essential is that we help one another create a new vision so that each person in the family has an opportunity to grow to his or her fullest potential.

Co-Parenting as the Solution

Throughout our history we have not been able to separate child-bearing from child-rearing. This has therefore limited our ability to notice that the care of the infant is its initiation rite into humanness and therefore any human can do it. For many reasons we women have participated in keeping mothering our own special experience. By doing this we have allowed ourselves to be limited to our unconscious power over infants without fully recognizing that there would be consequences to our behavior. What we have done is to forfeit real power for unconscious power. In contrast to what we have done, men have limited themselves to the power that comes through molding external events at the expense of learning how to be caring and nurturing human beings.[88]

Inviting men, even urging them into the nursery, will create problems for women. "Most of us, no matter what else we feel, still hang onto the belief that the mother-child tie is in some sense sacred. Whatever else it may be, it is clearly the most fundamental, universal, biologically sturdy tie we have. It has been a cornerstone, a pillar of human experience."[89] Being in the primary position in the lives of their children is not going to be given up lightly by women—and certainly not until they have something as sure and as fulfilling in the outside world.

Psychotherapist Leah Schaefer gives some additional support to the fact that women are not the only ones who can parent well. She states: "A lot of people, and this includes men, do like to take care of small, dependent people. . . . I've come to believe what is ordinarily called the maternal instinct is just the simple liking to take care of smaller creatures. Some human beings do not like it at all. It is not some biological imperative, which if frustrated will ruin or impoverish a woman's life. . . . I wouldn't be surprised if men were born with about the same capacity as women to care for and nurture children, except for the obvious biological differences."[90]

For centuries women have been defined by the biological function of reproduction. If we can separate reproduction from mothering, we can expand our sexual identity to include other aspects of femaleness. It is important that we learn to see mother as an ordinary human being. The best way that women can do this is to recognize that any human can parent small children. If we can finally admit this to ourselves we will transform the magic of mothering into a skilled and sensitive task. "When we become free enough to see mother, and, later on, father, as an ordinary person, we can begin to appreciate the gifts mother gave us and enjoy them. Consequently we would also be freed to recognize what she did not give us and begin to turn to others for what was missing. By placing mother in a new perspective we can release ourselves as well."[91]

By sharing this very special experience with men, we would be opening up a multitude of new experiences for ourselves. One of the most valuable benefits to women would come from the transference of negative feelings men have expressed for women for centuries as part of their resentment at being excluded from child rearing.

It is important to remember that exclusive mothering by one isolated woman is the historical exception and not the rule. There are whole cultures with extended households and various kinds of shared parenting. There are whole classes who have been raised by nurses. Clinical and autobiographical evidence suggests that in those classes where nurses reared children, it was often a warm, loving nurse who provided the bases for emotional capacities that distant, rejecting parents did not provide. One becomes a person in relation to stable, caring others, and such commitment may be made by biological or non-biological parents.[92]

Women will still have to deal with the problem of guilt because the mother who does not spend all day at home with her children because she cannot stand the isolation may continue to think that she is a bad mother. Society still expects the pre-school child's mother to stay at home. Her husband may encourage her to do what she wants but he may still wonder if some women could not handle being a mother better than his wife. It would be reassuring to women if they knew that the truth of the matter is that it is an impossible job for all women as it is presently defined.[93]

I tell parents who come to see me with child-raising issues that a healthy parent is one who is constantly working himself or herself out of a job. As children get older it is important to release the parental hold on them so that they can learn how to become independent, autonomous young adults. Children who grow up still attached to "mother's apron strings" are a product of mothers who are unable to let their children go when appropriate to do so. This is usually due to the fact that these women believe that there is no encore to the role of mom. As a therapist, it is my goal to help these women see other options and to realize that there are exciting and growth-filled opportunities that await them outside of and in addition to motherhood. We can be good mothers and still have full lives of our own.

Perhaps the very best answer that I have ever heard to the question "What do children really need?" comes from a poem by Dorothy Law Nolte. She gives us a beautiful summation of what ingredients go into healthy parenting.

Children Learn What They Live

If a child lives with criticism,
    He learns to condemn.
If a child lives with hostility,
    He learns to fight.
If a child lives with ridicule,
    He learns to be shy.
If a child lives with shame,
    He learns to feel guilty.
If a child lives with tolerance,
    He learns to be patient.
If a child lives with encouragement,
    He learns confidence.
If a child lives with fairness,
    He learns justice.
If a child lives with security,
    He learns to have faith.
If a child lives with approval,
    He learns to like himself.
If a child lives with acceptance and friendship,
    He learns to find love in the world.

◆ 7 ◆

Is There Life After Motherhood?

The noblest and best of earth in every age have honored and revered Mother and motherhood. By voice and pen they have delighted in expressing heartfelt and loving tributes to Mother and to mother-love; to her who has given herself, ofttimes, from starlit dawn to midnight's silent hour in untiring service and devotion to the physical and spiritual needs of her family; who is respected by all men for her charity toward the fallen and oppressed; who is loved for the consolation and comfort and helpfulness extended to the sick and needy and unfortunate, and for her womanly honor and nobility of mind and heart; who is adored for her sweetness and gentleness and purity of life and character—she who has done so much to shape the lives of men and women for the things that are eternal; who is extolled for her tender compassion, her noble self-sacrifice, her boundless mother-love; who is exalted for her living hope and trust in God and in the King of Glory; and whom we glorify for her steadfastness and sublimity of faith which more nearly approaches the divine than anything else we know in life.

Genial, sunshiny, happy. Hers is life's sweetest and tenderest love, a love beautiful and loyal and true, love that never fails. A halo of purity resting on her saintly brow—her face abeam with joy the world cannot give nor take away. Such mothers, though uncrowned, are the real queens of earth.[94]

Reading such an idealized description of motherhood based on the Victorian model would lead to the conclusion that there is no life after motherhood. How can there be when one is expected to do and be all that is described above? What could women possibly do for an encore? It is certainly understandable why this vision could have a paralyzing effect on a woman's self-discovery of her own individual uniqueness. When would she possibly have time? And if she did find time, how could she live with the guilt of selfishly pursuing her own goals?

What puzzles me is, that women have not fought more tenaciously against such idealization. Certainly, part of the reason could be that such a role is imprinted in our unconscious mind via the archetype of the Good Mother and the fact that only women mother. But some other factor seems to be working to encourage women to cooperate and accept such a role.

Some women do not wish to see any changes in women's roles. There has been a long-standing conflict between women who preferred the sheltered protection of conventional marriage and those who wanted to participate in the work force. In the nineteenth and early twentieth century and even today in the 1980's, the most serious opponents of the Women's movement and the passage of the Equal Rights Amendment were and still are conventionally married women, secure in their dependence on their husbands.[95]

Career women and working mothers had been on the defensive. The dependent, feminine, home-centered housewife had been the one receiving the accolades while the women who insisted on pursuing their own interests, who left the home to take jobs, were severely criticized. "The homebody certainly did not have to defend herself. She was carrying out God's plan." My mother was such a woman. It was not until the middle of this century that a tip in the balance began. It began to be publicly recognized that women did have a right and even an obligation to participate in the labor force. As a result of this shift in perspective, a housewife's backlash began. Housewives began to feel that they were being put on the defensive and were begining to feel denigrated if they did not also enter the labor force.[96]

The real anguish today occurs among the women who do not really want to enter the labor force and who want to remain home, sheltered and protected. They feel put down, denigrated by the emphasis on autonomy among the avant-garde. These women were "friendly and compliant" as girls and avoided aggressive play. Such a woman now describes herself as very conventional, dependent and not at all competitive. "Her personality style is built on muting of self-assertion and aggression and affirmation of love, nurturance and self-sacrifice. Fearful of attenuating family relationships, she avoids employment. Motherhood is her focal life role and she derives a sense of purpose and vitality as well as some vicarious achievement satisfaction from her family. Despite all these apparent pluses, however, she currently is experiencing some distress, has low self-esteem and perceives herself as neither attractive to men nor especially competent."[97]

Jessie Bernard tells us that this type of woman was "wired for marriage" by the socialization she had undergone. When she went to a young man in the marriageable years, what she proposed in effect if not in words was something like the following: "Please father the two or three children I need for my self-fulfillment; support me while I bear them; support them until they are about eighteen years old and me for the rest of my life. In return I promise to take care of your personal needs as long as you live or until you can afford to relieve me and hire others to do so." This was the image of life which formed the young woman's mentality, her sexuality, her emotionality. She was set in that course from the moment she was born. It was the best she felt she could hope for. She got what she was socialized to want, even though in some cases she got it at enormous costs.[98]

I can really identify with the above because I was such a woman. I went from my father's house to my husband's house and my marriage contract was based on the above format. It wasn't until I was in my early thirties and had three children that my distress became evident. I did not dare show it because I had sacrificed so much for the existing norms and I felt I had to continue cherishing them. I, like the woman mentioned by Bernard, put up a charming front, smiling, cheerful, unassuming, self-deprecating, unthreatening and never dreaming of demanding anything—certainly not freedom.[99]

Simone de Beauvoir described the anguish that such people as myself experience when the Other wipes them out of existence, when they are no longer seen by the Other as human beings, or, for that matter, even seen at all. Women throughout their lives experience this blotting out as individual human beings by the Other. "The loveliness of their youthful bodies is seen but not the bewildered young woman inside; the husband's wife is seen, but not the intelligent woman who has ideas of her own that she would like to contribute to the dinner party discussion; the infant's mother is seen, but not the eager woman who still wants to exhibit her sketches; the school child's mother is seen, but not the restless woman who wants to go back to school herself. Only recently are we beginning to see the woman as well as the mother."[100]

Bernard believes that as long as the woman's-place-is-in-the-home ideology had secure support all around, even theological support, the women themselves did not have to bestir themselves. But when these women who had selected the housewife identity in middle adulthood felt themselves on the defensive, the arguments of some of them became crasser. The backlash was directed at the feminists. Didn't these feminists know that they were upsetting the applecart? "Arguments that seemed better unarticulated in the past now came to be verbalized, namely, that there were rich rewards in the traditional role. It was a bargain, whatever the price. Who wanted equality when women were doing so much better as housewives? Women really had it made. Women libber's were rocking a very comfortable boat."[101]

It is my belief that women didn't want to rock the boat because it is much easier to remain a child and let someone else take care of you than to struggle for independence in the harsh, competitive world. I am not saying that a housewife and mother does not work hard at what she does, and I certainly took the job very seriously and was quite conscientious. I just think it was easier for me than it has been pursuing a full-time career. But such dependence on another comes with its own price tag. The price was that I felt totally powerless in my marriage. All the time that I remained at home I had a vague feeling of uneasiness. I was insecure because I knew down deep that if I ever questioned my husband's decisions or judgments or ever went against them, there was a possibility that I might end up out on my own. I knew I wasn't prepared for such an occurrence.

It is my belief that as long as women are in relationships where they are dependent they must be cautious. This is the nature of the relationship between the powerful and the powerless. There is really a threat implied in every request. Sometimes it is intended and sometimes it is not. But it doesn't really matter because as long as the threat is possible, so long as one person has the power to deprive another of important life supports, the powerless one experiences request as demand.[102]

One of the crucial problems for women, according to Nancy Friday, is that females were taught to merge, to expect satisfaction and identity to come from first pleasing mother, and later from pleasing men, and marrying one of them. That kind of training and thinking does not permit much room or encouragement for the development of an independent autonomous self. "Not for independence, not for an apartment of our own, not for experimenting with jobs, careers, work, sex, men, but for this—this is what mother raised us to be good at: to live for, through, and protected by others. It makes us feel more at peace than anything we ever did for and by ourselves."[103]

Women's desire to subordinate themselves to a man is the pattern of dependency learned from mother. "To escape the feeling that she may be ornamental but nevertheless fundamentally valueless, she becomes the woman who is behind the successful man. She will not try on her own. But even as she succeeds, even as she makes the man more successful, more valuable, her own feelings of self-worth diminish. The bigger he gets, the more frightened she becomes that he will leave her, a nobody."[104]

The fear of freedom—which we dress up and call the need for security—is rooted in the unresolved half of us which is still a child, still looking for a man to replace the mother we never successfully left. As long as we have our need for symbiosis, we will not believe that we can make it on our own. "The child thinks that if she becomes too strong, too independent, mother will decide she can make it on her own and neglect her. We keep ourselves little. It means we must continue to live as a child: powerless."[105]

Change is difficult for everyone. Oftentimes we may be unhappy and discontented with our life but we find it safer to keep the status quo than to make changes and risk the unknown. We like to "hedge our bets." Some women choose to handle this dilemma by attempting to keep the benefits from both roles. They want freedom to make decisions and still be protected and provided for. Colette Dowling calls this "gender panic." She states:

> Women continue dominating the homemaker role, whether or not they have an outside career, because they still feel dependent on their husbands and need something—a service—with which to balance out the arrangement. It's the reason women invest more in the whole idea of family than men do—why, regardless of how many hours they may put in at the office, they continue cooking the family meals from scratch, toasting their own granola in the oven, stitching up quilts to match the children's wallpaper.
>
> The safety of marriage—of being loved and needed—can be a mixed blessing for the woman who feels the urge to do something on her own but is afraid. Any negative pressure from "him" can be neatly turned into an external distraction from her own inner fears. Work, especially if it's conceived of

as the pursuit of one's own personal development and not just "helping out with the bills," is a way of separating or individuating oneself. Thus it can be experienced as a "going away from the other"—scary business indeed. Better to hang back in "the marriage." "I really care about my family" becomes the rationale for a major retreat in life.

The exhaustion women are expressing now, in relation to their "double burden," is the result of conflict—the clash between wanting to hang on to the domestic security housebound women have always enjoyed and the desire to be free and self-fulfilling. This unresolved, and thus paralyzing, conflict breeds Gender Panic, keeps women in low-level jobs or work they've outgrown, and keeps them overextended at home.[106]

What has happened is that most women have not made a true decision about their lives. They try to maintain a situation in which they give up neither independence nor dependence. This process ends up in draining them of energy. Women lose their decision-making power when they deny responsibility for themselves.

It doesn't work for women to seek power by simply pleasing the men in their lives. It is hard to be content with the power one is able to achieve through association with a strong male. This results in women acting like children who believe that there is someone wiser and stronger who will guide them and take away their pain.

Few of us ever outgrow the yearning to be guided as we were when we were children, to be told what to do for our own good by someone powerful who knows better and will protect us. By simply rebelling against the power of mother and shifting our dependence from female authority to male authority, we have not tackled the problem. We have merely substituted the gender of the person in power. The problem that we have avoided is our deep-seated wish to be free and taken care of simultaneously. We have not learned how to outgrow that wish, nor how to begin the task of learning to take care of ourselves.[107]

Women need to take responsibility for themselves in order to avoid feeling victimized by the world. If a woman takes the position of victim, she loses power, but if she chooses to take responsibility for her life, then she also has the power to do something about what happens. This gives a person a feeling of potency.

Any woman who does not learn how to look after herself financially and emotionally is sabotaging herself as surely as if she set a time bomb off under her bed. It doesn't matter what her age or marital status is. Psychotherapist Penelope Russianoff advises women to be prepared. She states: "With the frequency of divorce nowadays, and the gap between the ages of death for men and women, every woman owes it to herself to learn to fend for herself financially. If she doesn't, she's exploitable—and only she, not society, not men, is responsible."[108]

Women need to stop using Motherhood as an excuse for remaining dependent. It can no longer be substantiated that being a good mother necessitates living through others and sacrificing full authentic adulthood in order to meet their needs. "If mothers cannot openly demonstrate to their children the potential they have for dealing with their own lives, how can they help their children deal with their possibilities? If mother is someone who has to put off a 'full life' until the children are grown up, how can that woman possibly encourage growth?"[109]

In Victorian times, a rough equality between the sexes existed until puberty; then post-World War I women were encouraged to lead free, interesting lives until they were married. Now the goals of larger society are open to women until they become mothers. "Moving beyond the paralyzing, romantic idealism of the motherhood mystique is the final frontier for women."[110] The use of the role of motherhood as a reason for women living inauthentic lives must be stopped for the good of women, men, children and all of society. The price to all of us is just too high. There must be a life after motherhood!

♦ 8 ♦

The Future of Motherhood

What will motherhood look like in the future? Will we be able to conquer the motherhood myth and move beyond it? According to Sebald, human relationships that are patterned strictly on gender identity have declined or been modified and the vicissitudes of history have begun to erode the sharp contours of masculine and feminine role distinctions. But he believes it would be chimerical to believe that it has reached any state of completion. "There have been modifications of the traditional sex role behavior, but the social fact is that profound distinctions are still with us and, most likely, will stay with us for a long, long time to come."[111]

An example that illustrates that traditional sex roles still prevail is in a 1974 polling: only twenty-nine percent of a national sample of Americans eighteen and over disagreed with the idea that "men in our society have certain responsibilities and women have others. This is the way it should be." Forty-seven percent agreed with the statement and twenty-seven percent had no strong opinion. This simply illustrates the tenacity with which cultural images enchain society and how extremely slow they are to change.[112]

Sebald believes that "Momism"will continue for another fifty or sixty years and will increase but then decrease in the distant future. His long-term optimism is based on his belief that social policy will have a chance to grow on the accumulated evidence about the Momistic drama. "Its effects will be made more visible, and eventually it will out wear the patience and tolerance of insightful individuals in all walks of life."[113]

In the near future Momism will be a growing phenomenon in American society despite the increasing recognition and preventive attention paid to it by middle-class people. There appears to be an interesting shift in the life-style of the middle class, on one side, and the working class on the other. While the middle class shows symptoms of attempting to break out from a number of the pathological conditions of urban-industrial life (through part-time farming, the commune experience of the young, outdoor emphases, ecological concerns, innovative social policy, etc.), the working class shows all the symptoms of trying to emulate the customary middle-class life style. "It is yearning to get where the pathological action is: to adopt—unadulterated—the urban, industrial middle-class life-style, which all too frequently is characterized by Momism. Since many more blue-collar parents will enter the Momism-prone middle-class life style and fewer white-collar parents will leave it, more Momism will occur over the next two generations in American society."[114]

It is an historical truism that when a nouveau class ascends to a coveted social stratum, its imitation of the newly acquired social status is thorough and indiscriminate and thus we may expect, among other things, acquisition of the typical Momistic patterns.

"Momism for this nouveau middle class will be a by-product of the dubious blessings of technocracy, the father's absorption in an away-from-home career, and the mother's feeling of deprivation, her blind following of pseudo-scientific prescriptions for child rearing, and her use of the child as a success symbol. . . . All the conditions of Momism will be renewed and fortified by new waves of eager Moms. They are already in the wings, waiting to enter the stage and continue the drama of the Silent Disease. For two or three generations to come, there will be no end to the production of America's Moms."[115]

This nouveau middle class mom has been described as follows:

> The star of the Momistic drama of the nouveau middle class will be the young working-class woman (wife of the blue-collar worker), who numbers 40 million—almost 60% of all U.S. adult females. Customarily, her life centered around husband, children, and home. Now she is stirring restlessly, indicating dissatisfaction with her traditional life-style and the limited fate of being a housekeeper. She has received the message of liberation, although vaguely and indirectly. To her, liberation means a career or job outside the home with modern appliances, more "say" in family matters, and an enhanced sense of self-worth. This sense of self-worth is extremely touchy since it is new, not yet tested, and thus demands verification. Reassurance may be obtained through producing "top" offspring—and again we enter the vicious cycle of Momism: the child becomes the means for Mom's goals, particularly in situations where she has forgone or postponed a rewarding career away from home.
>
> While she is liberated from yesterday's house-

hold drudgery and confinement, she is somewhat confused. In a sense, she finds herself in a position of semi-retirement and, like retired individuals in general, looks for new goals and purposes to establish meaning for her life.

She is a delight to America's big business, developing confidence and shopping aggressiveness at a time when the middle-class woman is more and more alienated. She is less critical, more optimistic, and actively involved in improving her family's position. Her remarkable success in doing all this is a constant reinforcement for further pursuing the goods and services of our technocratic society. In the process, she is liberating herself from poverty, inadequate housing, shoddy furniture, mediocre clothes, and poor-quality food.

Most importantly, she is also liberating herself from the remnants of the extended family, in which her parents, grandparents, in-laws, or other relatives may have shared the household with her. With her mother or mother-in-law packing up and leaving, she has lost the live-in baby-sitter and is facing a new child-rearing pattern. She may decide to have fewer children (following "scientific" child-rearing advice) and stay home—at least temporarily—to launch her "motherhood career." These are the conditions that are all too often encountered along the familiar avenues of Momism.[116]

If this analysis is correct, then the near future is not promising. Social change takes time, and the road will be difficult for those women who wish to challenge the motherhood myth.

The Influences of Religion
on the Future of Motherhood

What role are conservative religions playing in preserving the motherhood myth? Sharon McIrvin Abu-Laban did an extensive study of this particular question. She mentions the fact that while a society may develop increasingly sophisticated and complex technology, this does not assure that it will move in the direction of increasing liberalization of values with a resulting liberation from traditional sex roles. To assume this underestimates the possibility of value confrontations or even reversals.[117]

Societal values and social movements are crucially relevant to predictions concerning women of the future. Abu-Laban notes the shifting religious climate in the United States as an example. There appears to be a return to traditional authoritarianism in American society arising from a base in "right-wing Protestant fundamentalism." The Gallup poll in a 1976 national survey reported some thirty-four percent of Americans indicating they had had the experience of being "born again." Another national sample reports that four out of ten Americans indicated that they had had some form of mystical religious experience. Membership in conservative churches has been growing at rates exceeding the growth of the general population.[118]

It is important to consider the extent to which contra-feminist movements are embedded in these expanding conservative religions. "While shifts away from religious rationalism need not be linked with paternalistic orientations toward women, the nexus between these groups and biblical literalism would appear to presage this role. In this perspective biblical writings are seen as the literal words of God and not (as in the more cosmopolitan, liberal, churches) fallible truths written by spiritually inspired humans. Religions which adhere to beliefs in biblical inerrancy tend to single out conservative passages regarding the female role, emphasizing the subordination of women and elevating patriarchal family patterns."[119]

The popular books *Fascinating Womanhood* and *Total Woman,* which we discussed at length in an earlier chapter, have emerged from conservative religious traditions (the Mormon and Southern Baptist, respectively). Furthermore, the significance of religious values is reflected in the fact that conservative religious backing and justification have been behind movements to defeat the Equal Rights Amendment. Such counter-movements, working to impose traditional values with respect to women's place and conduct, are likely to condemn and attempt to reverse the contemporary trends toward emancipating women.[120]

The potential power of an anti-feminist backlash, in combination with expanding conservative and fundamentalist religions, suggests neither increasing liberation from sex role ideologies, nor a projected maintenance of the status quo, but rather the possibility of a future return to a version of the status quo ante.[121]

"To the extent that contemporary, conservative religious movements embody restrictions which constrain women's access to prestige mechanisms other than those based on age-linked attractiveness or derived from a husband, to the extent that they restrict women to wife/ mother roles as the only meaningful and appropriate roles, then future women of advancing age will be exceptionally vulnerable to decline in status, and, as well,

vulnerable to several forms of socio-emotional deprivation."[122]

It is Abu-Laban's conclusion that the burgeoning
counterforce of religious conservatism, particularly when
fueled by less cerebral "faiths of the heart," have impli-
cations which will embody elements of "heartlessness"
for future generations of women. Should contemporary
conservative forces gain headway with respect to tradi-
tionalist prescriptions and proscriptions regarding females, the future of aging women may hold striking
similarities to the interpersonal, prestige, power, and
financial inequities experienced by the older women of
today.[123]

Perhaps the return to religious conservatism and the
resulting restriction of roles for women is another example of the "Good Mother" archetype. Just when we seem
to be making tremendous strides forward in augmenting
women's roles, we are once again pushed backward by
the pull of the unconscious. It may well be that any
future progress for women will depend on our ability to
move beyond this archetype.

The "Good Mother" Archetype: Can it Change?

In a lecture given to the C. G. Jung Institute of San
Francisco entitled "Archetypes—Eternal or Evolving?"
psychologist June Singer speculated about this possibility.
She asks the question: "If humanity has changed so much
over time are we to believe that today is the culmination
of what will always be?" Humans today are a link in a
very long chain of evolution that is continuing to evolve.

Recently we have broken through boundaries that have limited human beings for tens of thousands of years. It is as though evolution has suddenly speeded up, and Singer sees new possibilities for the future as being forever present.[124]

Singer quotes the work of Dr. Rupert Sheldrake who is the author of *A New Science of Life: The Hypothesis of Formative Causation.* She looks to Sheldrake's work for some answers. He states that animals are tuned into a certain patterning. Turtles hatch in the sand and know to run to the sea before they are caught by predators. Birds know just where and when to migrate. This is not learned behavior. According to Sheldrake, patterning gets stronger the more a certain behavior happens. The tendency to reproduce behavior becomes strengthened the more it is done. The more we behave in a certain way the more likely it is to become a pattern.[125]

If archetypes are based on non-learned behavior and are patterns, perhaps they can change also. A good example of how patterning can change is given in the story about the "one hundredth monkey." There were monkeys on the coast of Japan eating sweet potatoes with lots of dirt on them. One day a young monkey suddenly conceived of the idea of going down to the seashore and washing his potato. His parents observed him and also began to wash their sweet potatoes and seemed to like it. Soon others did the same. There came to be a point when, symbolically speaking, the one hundredth monkey washed his potato. Then, on another island far away, the monkeys there also began washing their sweet potatoes.[126]

Sheldrake would explain this phenomenon by his theory of morphic resonance. There is a "tuning in" that happens at a certain point when the signals get loud enough that it is possible to tune into a patterning process and go with it. When the first monkey began washing his sweet potato he also began washing a little channel in the collective unconscious. A pattern of behavior began to be slightly modified. When that happened over and over again that pattern became more deeply canalized. The more that it happened the more it was likely to happen in the future.[127]

When something new happens it gets incorporated in our way of functioning both consciously and unconsciously. When patterns become incorporated in the unconscious of sufficient numbers of people, animals or plant life, they become incorporated into that species' unconscious pattern. The pattern itself is thus affected. The patterning gets stronger and stronger the more a behavior happens. The tendency to reproduce behavior becomes strengthened the more people do it.[128]

If what Singer and Sheldrake are saying is true, then perhaps there is hope for the future of women. It is Singer's belief that archetypes are not just sitting there but changing also. They are evolving and not merely static. The archetype of the "Great Mother Goddess" is changing albeit slowly. That archetype was necessary in an age when it was imperative for a species' survival that females parented children while males who were physically larger hunted for food and provided shelter and protection from predators. It is understandable that early man, with his magical thinking, would be overwhelmed and frightened by the female's power to create life. But a new archetype is necessary for today's world and now is imperative for our survival as a species.

What we need is a new vision of motherhood that will free women to be whole, integrated human beings. It is also to the benefit of men that this vision be realized.

Shared parenthood would allow men an opportunity to develop their nurturing capacities. An integrated adult is both masculine and feminine, and it is precisely this highly developed individual that is now needed in order to insure the future of humankind.

Women Meeting The Challenge

There are some women today who are attempting to live out a new vision of motherhood. They have no role models for how to do this and certainly they have little support from society. These are very courageous women who struggle to grow beyond the confines of women's existing roles. They try out new ways of acting and while doing so they risk a great deal. Resistance to change is enormous, and these women find themselves very alone in their struggle to be more than they presently are. They remind me of the first little monkey who went to the seashore to wash his potato. Someone has to be willing to risk ridicule, criticism and condemnation in order to try out a new kind of behavior. These women have a vision of a better way of living, and that vision gives them the courage to move forward in spite of the enormous conflicts this causes them personally. Hopefully, other women will follow their example and a new pattern for women will be established.

What we now need is a new balance of personality characteristics that include those of each sex. The new balance would not call for a diminution of the virtues of either sex but for sharing of both sets of virtues by both sexes. "For just as the major defect in the Victorian model for the role of mother was its exaggeration of the nurturant virtues at the almost total expense of strength, so also the major defect of macho has been the exaggeration of the power component at the almost total expense of tenderness and gentleness."[129]

This new balance is not necessarily going to be utopia and it is not threatening us with matriarchy. The Great Mother is not going to take over. But the qualities she symbolizes will be shared by more and more men. Both children and the social order will profit by opening up motherhood for men to share. The old balance was too restrictive and will not work in this day and age. It did not make room for the male strengths required of mothers and it did not extend nurturant virtues to fathers. "Western humankind" must arrive at a synthesis that includes the feminine world. Only then will the individual human being be able to develop the psychic wholeness that is urgently needed if Western Man is to face the dangers that threaten his existence from within and without. We really can no longer afford to deprive either sex of the strength of the other. "Motherhood is too important to leave to women alone."[130]

Hopefully, as women grow and develop in a more healthy manner, motherhood, as we now know it, will undergo a major transformation. This change will have dramatic behavioral and psychological effects on men, women, and children. I can envision a time when co-parenting is the accepted norm. Our traditional system in which the mother is in charge of child-rearing and the father is seen as the distant or unavailable parent causes boys and girls to grow up with an unconscious image of the mother as an omnipotent and consequently somewhat fearful figure. This image evokes hostility from both sexes but especially from males who must undergo a greater separation process in the evolution of their eventual identification with the male gender.[131]

Maternal child care results in excess psychological baggage that reinforces the patriarchal society. When child care becomes a sexually shared responsibility we will see a decline in sexual stereotyping. This would result in less resentment of women by men since boys would be less likely to view their mothers as omnipotent and so have less cause to develop immature fears to carry into adulthood. "A biological mother will, by the force of nature, infant bonding, and the maternal relationship, remain a primary influence but the scope of that influence would be subject to change. The mother would still be in a position to shape her children's perceptions of the world, but children's perceptions would be significantly different due to co-parenting with males."[132]

I envision a future where women will no longer view marriage as their primary source of status and economic support. Women will marry for healthier reasons. A woman who finds that her relationship with a man is undermining her sense of self-esteem, or if he is psychologically or physically abusive to her, will not consider it necessary to cling to a relationship for the traditional reasons, and she will have the self-sufficiency to stand on her own.

Women of the future will have the ability to control their child-bearing more carefully, and consequently men will no longer be able to take it for granted that fatherhood is their natural right. A society of self-supporting women will be able to evaluate a man's appropriateness as a father on terms that will include more emphasis on the father as an emotional rather than financial provider. Men who do not appear to fit this criterion will not be chosen by women as fathers for their children. This will be a powerful motivator for men to change their traditional behavior patterns. As men begin to change they will see many additional benefits to themselves as well.[133]

It is my belief that such a future is possible, but whether it becomes a reality is dependent on women themselves. It will take a tremendous amount of courage to risk making the necessary changes. Trying out new behavior will cause a great deal of internal conflict. But if we understand how necessary it is that we move forward in spite of the conflict, we will find the strength to break through the barriers that are presently retarding our growth.

It is much too easy to blame the current inequities on men or society. We women contribute to our own weakness and vulnerability. We actually nourish and defend our inner dependencies. "But the more we are able to face down our conflicts and seek our own solutions the more inner freedom and strength we will gain. It is when we assume responsibility for our own problems that the center of gravity begins to make that crucial shift from the Other to the Self."[134]

There are women today who are creatively finding a new definition of womanhood. These women will offer themselves as role models for the women of tomorrow. As women's behavior changes, so will the patterning in our unconscious. We can change the archetype from "Good Mother Goddess" to "Fully Functioning, Integrated, Human Adult Mother." Such a future is possible and women of tomorrow will no longer be plagued by the question: Motherhood: What do I do for an encore? Their lives will be their answer.

Conclusion

Having done a great deal of research on women's issues, I find myself being a guest lecturer on many occasions speaking to women. In the past I have often been asked at these lectures if I believe women should have a choice of whether they stay home and raise their family or go out and join the work force. I have been very reluctant to say that women did not have a choice because I didn't want to be seen as inflexible and rigid in my views. So I usually side-stepped the issue by saying that women could choose to remain at home if they were at the same time developing transferable skills to use in the job market. I was giving them the message to "hedge their bets." I was not saying how I really felt about the issue out of my own timidity and fear.

I am now a few years older and wiser and have seen with my own eyes the problems facing today's women. When I am now asked the same question regarding women's choices I emphatically state that I no longer believe that there is a real choice for women. I believe that it is self-destructive for any woman not to have the ability to support herself financially. Women used to feel that if they had a college education they were secure, but in today's world you need recent job training and experience. A college graduate who hasn't worked in fifteen years will find herself with a job that pays little more than minimum wage. It is crucially important that women know these facts before they choose to stay home and be full-time mothers.

Colette Dowling is very right when she tells us that the "Cinderella Complex" is alive and well. "Personal, psychological dependency—the deep wish to be taken care of by others—is the chief force holding women down today. Women have repressed attitudes and fears that keep them in a kind of half-light, retreating from the full use of their minds and creativity. Like Cinderella, women today are still waiting for something external to transform their lives."[135]

The reality of the external world has changed significantly since even my own mother's time. My mother could choose to stay home with her children and become the woman behind the man. Divorce was not nearly so prevalent even one generation ago. Several generations ago this choice was viable because if your husband died or left, you had extended family to rely on for support. But today divorce is at its all-time high, families are isolated and the possibility that a woman will have to stand on her own is quite high indeed. The choice for women is no longer there.

Statistics support my stance. The divorce rate in California is now over fifty percent. In fact, forty-seven percent of all California women are widowed or divorced, and there has been an increase of forty-six percent in the number of female-headed households in the last ten years. In cases of divorce, the California law requires that community property be divided equally. Although this law appears to be equitable in nature, its fairness is illusory in practice. In almost all cases, the most substantial asset of the marriage is not the home or the savings account or the automobile. Rather, it is the husband's earning power, and this is never equally divided.[136]

What has happened is that during the marriage the husband pursued his career and the wife did not, or, if she did, it came second to his. When divorce occurs the woman must rely on her own ability to make a living. Only ten percent of women nationwide will receive any spousal support. The woman oftentimes has to take a job at minimum wage. This is hardly enough to live decently.

I think that it is important that women know that it has been said that "every woman is only one man away from welfare." In California, seventy-five percent of all welfare recipients are women.[137] The annual income of families headed by displaced homemakers rarely exceeds five thousand dollars. Only twenty-one percent of women receive any child support payments, with payments averaging just over two hundred dollars a month. These statistics prove that women are in a very precarious position indeed.[138A]

Quoting such statistics may be viewed by some as scare tactics but I don't think so. What I am saying is reality. It doesn't matter whether one is divorced or not—all women have these problems to face. Reality hits hard when the men die off. The latest government figures show fifty-six to be the average age of widowhood in the United States. Over one out of two women can expect to be a widow by the age of sixty-five. Even those women who spend their adult lives working are not protected in old age; one out of four of them will be poor. In 1977, the median income of all older females was

$3,087 compared with a median income for older males of almost twice that.[138B]

"This then, is the bitter truth on which younger women—still romantic, still in love, still cushioned by the dream that women can safely allow others to take care of them—turn their backs. The myth is that security, for women, lies in remaining forever and permanently attached, coiled within and stuck to the family like mollusks within their shells. But by the time these same women grow older, they are horribly disenfranchised, snapped off from the main economy before they know what hit them."[139]

Dowling believes that the devastation of old age is the most poignant outcome of the Cinderella complex, if not the most destructive. "It is tantamount to a kind of sickness, this blind spot we maintain—the inability (or refusal) to see the connection between the false security we connect with being wives and the loneliness and poverty of older often widowed women. We want so desperately to believe that someone else will take care of us. We want so desperately to believe that we do not have to be responsible for our own welfare."[140]

The myth is particularly prevalent among women of the middle class. They wear rose-colored glasses and see work as a kind of experiment, a form, almost of play. They languish in part-time jobs that they think will "brighten their horizons" or allow them "to get out of the house and meet people." They depend on others for security.

I met such a woman recently. I was up at Lake Tahoe, California for a few days of rest and relaxation. I went to a cocktail show to see a famous entertainer. Sitting next to me at the same table was a lovely couple.

The husband was a financially successful man working for an electronics company in Santa Clara County (also known as Silicon Valley, California's famous home of companies making semi-conductor devices). The first thing the wife asked me was how many children I had and what they were doing. Her whole conversation was about children. Now, this is an attractive, very intelligent, charming woman who is capable of doing anything she wants in life. It was as if, for her, nothing else existed outside of motherhood.

As I conversed with this woman I found myself feeling quite angry. I wanted to shake her and tell her one of my horror stories (of which I have many) of a displaced homemaker. I wanted to tell her about Mary, who was fifty-eight years old and from Kentucky. She had been married for forty years and had come out to California with her husband for their daughter's wedding. When they got to their daughter's house the husband took her suitcases out of the car and placed them on the sidewalk. He told her he was returning to Kentucky without her because he was in love with a younger woman and they wanted to get married. He subsequently returned to Kentucky and filed for divorce, leaving the wife in California to fend for herself. Mary had no money and no job skills, since she had never worked outside of the home. She had no money for an attorney to protect her legal rights. She was in a totally dependent situation and her plight was sad indeed. This story is not as rare as one would like to think.

I could have told this story to my new-found friend but it was not appropriate to do so, and I doubt that she would have heard me anyway. Some of my anger was toward her, but some was toward myself as well. I had a real sense of déjà vu as I watched this couple. I, too, had believed that my security depended on a man, and I was quite shocked when my husband wanted out of our marriage. I remembered believing that such a thing would never happen to me. I, like my friend, was a protected one: young, attractive, sassy—and safe. I presumed financial dependence to be my right, as a woman. In exchange I devoted myself to homemaking, happily priding myself in my ability to clean, to organize, to rear children, to entertain. Inwardly, without being conscious of it, I, too, had set up an agenda: I avoided, almost ritualistically, any recognition of how precarious my life was. I did not think about what would happen if my marriage were to break up. Divorce happens, of course. I saw it all around me. But I never imagined it happening to me. It was for others, for women who were not quite so fortunate—like cancer, or death.[141]

Colette Dowling expresses it well when she tells us that women today are caught in a cross-fire between old and radically new social ideas, but the truth is that we cannot fall back on the old "role" anymore. "It's not functional; it's not a true option. We may think it is; we may want it to be; but it isn't. The prince has vanished. The caveman has grown smaller and weaker. In fact, in terms of what is required for survival in the modern world, he is really no stronger, or smarter, or more courageous than we are. He is, however, more experienced."[142]

Life is offering today's woman a tremendous challenge, and I believe we women have the courage to face it head-on. No relationship, whether it be with husband or child, can last forever. Our self-identities can no longer be premised on the health of our relationships to others. We can no longer depend on relationships to tell us who we are and to supply us with a reason for being.

Husbands may leave or die, and children do grow up and move away. These are facts of life, and it proves to us how important it is that we have an identity outside of our mother and wife roles.

It will only be when women have a new vision of motherhood that we will have an opportunity to self-actualize. Abraham Maslow defines self-actualization as actualization of potentials, capacities and talents and the fulfillment of a mission (or call, fate, destiny, or vocation). It is a fuller knowledge of, and acceptance of, the person's own intrinsic nature. In the process of self-actualization there is an unceasing trend toward unity, integration or synthesis within the person.[143] Therefore, if a woman is to be capable of this process she must see herself as more than just simply a wife and mother. She must become all that she can be. Limiting oneself to these roles in the belief that it is the "right" or "correct" thing to do is modern-day woman's biggest mistake. It causes women to be dependent on relationships to others for self-definition, and this is counter-productive to the self-actualization process. Women being kept dependent like children really benefits no one.

I have always thought of myself as a visionary and see tremendous possibilities for women in the years ahead. I believe in women and in our ability to open our eyes and see clearly the essential need to create for ourselves our own encore for motherhood. As we are given the opportunity to grow and prosper, we will find that being afraid of change need not hold us back and that our new-found inner strength and security will be well worth the struggle.

After a while you learn the subtle difference
Between holding a hand and chaining a soul,

And you learn that love doesn't mean leaning
And company doesn't mean security,
And you begin to learn that kisses aren't contracts
And presents aren't promises,
And you begin to accept your defeats
With your head up and your eyes open,
With the grace of a woman, not the grief of a child,
And learn to build all your roads
On today because tomorrow's ground
Is too uncertain for plans, and futures have
A way of falling down in mid-flight.
After a while you learn that even sunshine
Burns if you get too much.
So you plant your own garden and decorate
Your own soul, instead of waiting
For someone to bring you flowers.
And you learn that you really can endure . . .
That you really are strong
And you really do have worth.
And you learn and learn . . .
With every goodbye you learn.

Comes the Dawn
Anonymous

Notes

1. Lillian Rubin, *Intimate Strangers* (New York: Harper & Row, 1983), p. 56.

2. *Ibid.*, p. 59.

3. *Ibid.*

4. *Ibid.*, p. 177.

5. *Ibid.*, p. 196.

6. *Ibid.*

7. Jessie Bernard, *The Future of Motherhood* (New York: Dial Press Inc., 1974), p. 7.

8. *Ibid.*, p. 8.

9. *Ibid.*

10. *Ibid.*, p. 9.

11. *Ibid.*

12. *Ibid.*, p. 10.

13. *Ibid.*, p. 11.

14. *Ibid.*, p. 12.

15. *Ibid.*

16. *Ibid.*

17. *Ibid.*, p. 79.

18. *Ibid.*, p. 356.

19. *Ibid.*, p. 357.

20. *Ibid.*, p. 361.

21. Adrienne Rich, *Of Woman Born* (New Jersey: W. W. Norton & Co., Inc., 1976), p. 115.

22. *Ibid.*

23. E. O. James, *The Cult of the Mother Goddess* (New York: Frederich A. Praeger, 1959), p. 229.

24. Erik Neumann, *The Great Mother* (New Jersey: Princeton University Press, 1955), p. 3.

25. *Ibid.*, p. 4.

26. *Ibid.*, p. 5.

27. *Ibid.*, p. 11.

28. *Ibid.*

29. *Ibid.*, p. 12.

30. *Ibid.*, p. 15.

31. Maria Herrera-Sobek, "The Treacherous Woman Archetype: A Structuring Agent in the Corrido," *Azlan*, Vol. 13 (Spring-Fall 1982), p. 137.

32. *Ibid.*, p. 139.

33. *Ibid.*, p. 140.

34. Jane Flax, "A Materialist Theory of Women's Status," *Psychology of Women Quarterly*, Vol. 6, No. 1 (1981), p. 129.

35. Dorothy Dinnerstein, *The Mermaid and the Minotaur* (New York: Harper & Row, 1977), p. 112.

36. Rich, p. 110.

37. Hans Sebald, *Momism: The Silent Disease of America* (Chicago: Nelson Hall Co., 1976), p. 4.

38. *Ibid.*, p. 5.

39. *Ibid.*

40. *Ibid.*, p. 7.

41. *Ibid.*

42. *Ibid.*, p. 9.

43. *Ibid.*, p. 34.

44. *Ibid.*

45. *Ibid.*, p. 22.

46. Angela Barron McBride, *The Growth and Development of Mothers* (New York: Harper & Row, 1973) , p. 133.

47. *Ibid.*

48. *Ibid.*, p. 135.

49. Sebald, p. 23.

50. *Ibid.*, p. 27.

51. *Ibid.*, p. 28.

52. *Ibid.*, p. 29.

53. *Ibid.*, p. 30.

54. *Ibid.*

55. *Ibid.*, p. 40.

56. Irene Claremont de Castillejo, *Knowing Woman* (New York: Harper & Row, 1973), p. 42.

57. Sebald., p. 41.

58. *Ibid.*, p. 235.

59. *Ibid.*, pp. 124–127.

60. *Ibid.*, p. 129.

61. *Ibid.*, p. 16.

62. *Ibid.*, p. 17.

63. *Ibid.*

64. Martha L. Rogers, "Fascinating Womanhood as a Regression in the Emotional Maturation of Women," *Psychology of Women Quarterly,* Vol. 2, No. 3 (1978), p. 204.

65. *Ibid.*, p. 205.

66. *Ibid.*

67. Colette Dowling, *The Cinderella Complex: Women's Hidden Fear of Independence* (New York: Simon & Schuster, 1981), p. 156.

68. *Ibid.*

69. Rogers, p. 205.

70. McBride, p. 10.

71. Rogers, p. 208.

72. Dowling, p. 59.

73. Rogers, p. 213.

74. Barbara Powell, "The Empty Nest, Employment, and Psychiatric Symptoms in College-Educated Women," *Psychology of Women Quarterly,* Vol. 2, No. 1 (Fall 1977), p. 35.

75. *Ibid.*, p. 36.

76. *Ibid.*, p. 42.

77. Dorothy Kaufman McCall, "Simone de Beauvoir, The Second Sex, and Jean-Paul Sartre," *Signs: Journal of Women in Culture and Society,* Vol. 5, No. 2 (1979), p. 216.

78. *Ibid.,* p. 212.
79. Claire Etaugh, "Effects of Nonmaternal Care on Children," *American Psychologist,* Vol. 35, No. 4 (1980), p. 309.
80. *Ibid.,* p. 311.
81. *Ibid.*
82. *Ibid.,* p. 312.
83. *Ibid.,* p. 316.
84. Nancy Chodorow, *The Reproduction of Mothering* (Berkeley: University of California Press, 1978), p. 217.
85. Sebald, pp. 262–263.
86. *Ibid.,* pp. 243–245.
87A. *Ibid.,* p. 245.
87B. *Ibid.,* pp. 249–250.
88. Joan Hammerman Robbins, "Breaking the Taboos: Further Reflections on Mothering," *Journal of Humanistic Psychology,* Vol. 20, No. 2 (Spring 1980), p. 32.
89. *Ibid.,* p. 33.
90. *Ibid.,* p. 34.
91. *Ibid.*
92. Judith Lorber, Rose Laub Coser, Alice S. Rossi, and Nancy Chodorow, "On the Reproduction of Mothering: A Methodological Debate," *Signs: Journal of Women in Culture and Society,* Vol. 6, No. 3 (1981), p. 513.
93. McBride, p. 141.
94. Bernard, p. 5.
95. Jessie Bernard, *Women, Wives and Mothers: Values and Options* (Chicago, Ill.: Aldine Publishers, 1975), p. 118.
96. *Ibid.,* p. 119.
97. *Ibid.*
98. *Ibid.*
99. *Ibid.,* p. 120.
100. *Ibid.,* p. 104.
101. *Ibid.,* p. 122.
102. Lillian Rubin, *Women of a Certain Age* (New York: Dell Publishing Co., Inc., 1978), p. 345.

103. Robbins, p. 36.

104. *Ibid.*

105. Nancy Friday, *My Mother/My Self* (New York: Dell Publishing Co., Inc., 1978), p. 345.

106. Dowling, p. 209.

107. Robbins, p. 36.

108. Penelope Russianoff, *Why Do I Think I Am Nothing Without a Man?* (New York: Bantam Books, Inc. 1982), p. 136.

109. McBride, p. 149.

110. *Ibid.*

111. Sebald, p. 283.

112. *Ibid.*

113. *Ibid.*, p. 284.

114. *Ibid.*, p. 285.

115. *Ibid.*, p. 286.

116. *Ibid.*, p. 287.

117. Sharon McIrwin Abu-Laban, "Women and Aging: A Futurist Perspective," *Psychology of Women Quarterly*, Vol. 6, No. 1 (Fall 1981), p. 93.

118. *Ibid.*, p. 94.

119. *Ibid.*

120. *Ibid.*

121. *Ibid.*

122. *Ibid.*, p. 95.

123. *Ibid.*, p. 96.

124. June Singer, "Archetypes—Eternal or Evolving?" Lecture given to the C. G. Jung Institute of San Francisco, 1982.

125. *Ibid.*

126. *Ibid.*

127. *Ibid.*

128. *Ibid.*

129. Bernard, *The Future of Motherhood*, p. 364.

130. *Ibid.*, p. 365.

131. Laura Ashcraft and Elizabeth Nickles, *The Coming Matriarchy* (New York: Berkeley Books, Inc., 1981), p. 180.

132. *Ibid.*, p. 181.

133. *Ibid.*, p. 186.

134. Dowling, p. 235.

135. *Ibid.*, p. 21.

136. Joint Committee on Legal Equality, "Facts About California Women."

137. *Ibid.*

138A. U.S. Dept. of Labor, Bureau of Labor Statistics; Displaced Homemakers Network, Inc.

138B. Dowling, p. 40.

139. *Ibid.*, p. 41.

140. *Ibid.*

141. *Ibid.*, p. 44.

142. *Ibid.*, p. 16.

143. Abraham Maslow, *Toward a Psychology of Being* (New York: D. Van Nostrand Co., 1968), p. 25.

Bibliography

A. Books

Ashcraft, Laura and Nickles, Elizabeth, *The Coming Matriarchy.* New York: Berkeley Books, Inc., 1981.

Bernard, Jessie. *The Future of Motherhood.* New York: Dial Press Inc., 1974.

———. *Women, Wives and Mothers: Values and Options.* Chicago., Ill.: Aldine Publishers, 1975.

Chodorow, Nancy. *The Reproduction of Mothering.* Berkeley: University of California Press, 1978.

Dinnerstein, Dorothy. *The Mermaid and the Minotaur—Sexual Arrangements and Human Malaise.* New York: Harper & Row, 1977.

Friday, Nancy. *My Mother/My Self.* New York; Dell, 1978.

James, E. O. *The Cult of the Mother Goddess.* New York: Frederich A. Praeger, 1959.

Maslow, Abraham. *Toward a Psychology of Being.* New York: D. Van Nostrand Co., 1968.

McBride, Angela Barron. *The Growth and Development of Mothers.* New York: Harper & Row, 1973.

106

Neumann, Erik. *The Great Mother.* New Jersey: Princeton University Press, 1955.

Rich, Adrienne. *Of Woman Born.* New Jersey: W. W. Norton & Co. Inc., 1976.

Rothman, Sheila M. *Woman's Proper Place.* New York: Basic Books, 1978.

Rubin, Lillian B. *Intimate Strangers.* New York: Harper & Row, 1983.

————. *Women of a Certain Age.* New York: Harper & Row, 1979.

Russianoff, Penelope. *Why Do I Think I Am Nothing Without a Man?* New York: Bantam Books, Inc., 1982.

Sebald, Hans. *Momism: The Silent Disease of America.* Chicago: Nelson Hall Co., 1976.

B. Articles

Etaugh, Claire. "Effects of Nonmaternal Care on Children," *American Psychologist* 35 (1980), pp. 309–319.

Flax, Jane. "A Materialist Theory of Women's Status," *Psychology of Women Quarterly* 6 (Fall 1981), pp. 123–135.

Herrera-Sobek, Maria. "The Treacherous Woman Archetype: A Structuring Agent in the Corrido," *Azlan* 13 (Spring-Fall 1982), pp. 135–148.

Lorber, Judith, Coser, Rose Laub, Rossi, Alice S., and Chodorow, Nancy. "On the Reproduction of Mothering: A Methodological Debate," *Signs: Journal of Women in Culture and Society* 6 (1981), pp. 482–514.

McCall, Dorothy Kaufmann. "Simone de Beauvoir, The Second Sex, and Jean-Paul Sartre," *Signs: Journal of Women in Culture and Society* 5 (1979), pp. 209–222.

McIrwin Abu-Laban, Sharon. "Woman and Aging: A Futurist Perspective," *Psychology of Women Quarterly* 6 (Fall 1981), pp. 85–96.

Powell, Barbara. "The Empty Nest, Employment, and Psychiatric Symptoms in College-Educated Women," *Psychology of Women Quarterly* 2 (Fall 1977), pp. 35–44.

Robbins, Joan Hammerman. "Breaking the Taboos: Further Reflections on Mothering" *Journal of Humanistic Psychology* 20 (Spring 1980), pp. 27–40.

Rogers, Martha L. "Fascinating Womanhood as a Regression in the Emotional Maturation of Women," *Psychology of Women Quarterly* 2 (Spring 1978), pp. 202–213.